# THE GOD OF MIRACLES

Printed and bound by Lightning Source UK, Milton Keynes

Published by Crossbridge Books
Tree shadow, Berrow Green
Martley WR6 6PL
Tel: 01886 821128
© CROSSBRIDGE BOOKS 2004

First published 2004

ISBN 0 9543573 3 7

British Library Cataloguing in Publication Data. A catalogue
record for this book is available from the British Library.

Also by Trevor Dearing:

*Supernatural Superpowers* (Logos/Bridge USA)
*Supernatural Healing Today* (Logos/Bridge USA)
*God and Healing of the Mind* (Bridge/Valley)
*A People of Power* (Marshall Collins)
*It's True!* (Mohr Books)
*Total Healing* (Mohr Books)

Also by Anne Dearing:

*Called to Be a Wife* (Crossbridge Books)

# THE GOD OF MIRACLES

## TREVOR AND ANNE DEARING

## CROSSBRIDGE BOOKS

# *Dedicated*

to the glory of God
and in memory of
Ted and Hilda,
Trevor's dear parents

# Acknowledgements

We would like to thank our publisher, Mrs Eileen Mohr, for the enormous amount of work she has done in assembling the material presented in this book, and for her most helpful contributions in editing it.

We want to thank all those who have encouraged and inspired us through recounting by letter or verbally to us how God has used us in their healing, conversion and the spiritual enrichment of their lives.

We trust that giving their stories wider publicity will likewise encourage faith and blessing in those who now read them.

T. and A.D.

# Contents

# Prologue

This is a book full of miracles of healing wrought by God the Father, in the name of His Son Jesus Christ, through the power of His Holy Spirit. It is an account of miracles especially wrought by God through His use of the ministries of Trevor Dearing and his wife Anne. These servants of God are sure that these miracles are only a *sample* of what God has done through their ministries, as letters arrive regularly at their home from people who have not shared the news of their particular miracle before.

Moreover, Trevor and Anne are frequently being told vocally by worshippers attending their healing meetings about what God did in the realm of the miraculous through their ministry, often many years ago. In fact Trevor and Anne's ministry has spanned thirty-three years, and has taken them all over the British Isles and to many countries in different parts of the world.

One thing they can say for sure, is that the miracles of healing have stood the test of time. In this book those who have received a miracle from God are, for the most part, telling of God's work in their lives in their own words; though sometimes, to maintain confidentiality, only their initials, or even a pseudonym are used. Verification is available from the authors for any doubters!

This is not a teaching book. Any who would like to study the subject of Divine Healing in depth, including such topics as why a lot of people do not receive God's healing miracle; the place of the medical profession in the purposes of God; the Biblical basis for the ministry, and how to minister

Divine Healing to the sick are invited to order Trevor's book *Total Healing* from Crossbridge Books. Also, this present book does by no means tell the whole story of Trevor's and Anne's experiences of God's grace and their ministry throughout their lives. Again, any who would like to read their life stories can contact Crossbridge Books for *It's True!* (Trevor's story) and *Called to Be a Wife* (Anne's story). Many have testified to the wonderful and deep inspiration and increase of faith which these books have brought to them. Trevor and Anne have heard of seekers after truth becoming Christians through reading them. They trust that you will find rich blessing as you read the remarkable accounts of God's work of love and power in this, Trevor's ninth, and Anne's second book.

# Introduction

"I am Gabriel and you are sent to heal the sick."

This was the awe-inspiring commission Trevor received in a vision on 10th May 1969 when, after a long period of prayer and fasting, he was receiving an indescribable infilling of the Holy Spirit. It was during this Divine visitation that he first spoke in "tongues" and sang the praises of God "in the Spirit".

That evening Anne had left Trevor in charge of the four children and they had, mercifully, all fallen asleep very quickly. Trevor had immediately given himself to another time of seeking the Lord.

When Anne entered the house after Trevor's momentous spiritual experience, she exclaimed:

"Trevor! Your face is glowing with light like a beacon. Where have you been?"

"To heaven and back!" was Trevor's joyous reply.

Trevor had, in fact, himself been miraculously healed at the age of nineteen of serious nervous and physical disorders which threatened to ruin or indeed shorten his life. It was when he had first encountered the living reality of Jesus in a Methodist Church in Hull, Yorkshire. He had subsequently undergone intensive Biblical and theological training at Cliff College in Derbyshire, Wesley College in Leeds and Queen's College in

Birmingham. He had served as a Methodist Minister, Anglican Curate and Vicar of two parishes. He had eventually, in 1969, witnessed Divine healing ministry at Hyde Valley Pentecostal Church in Welwyn Garden City – but had never imagined that one day he himself would actually be Divinely commissioned to minister to the sick. He did so at first as a guest speaker at Hyde Valley Pentecostal Church, where immediately ten sufferers testified to instantaneous healing. He continued this ministry as soon as he was appointed to be vicar of a small Anglican Church in Hainault, Essex, in September 1970. So many miracles of conversion, deliverance from evil spirits, and healings began to happen that soon thousands of people flocked to St Paul's, Hainault, from all over Britain and even from distant parts of the world. Trevor's work at Hainault became the subject of massive media coverage.

Anne, all this time, was an onlooker who nonetheless was in charge of counselling at the church. She had never known a time, from being very young, when God was not real to her and she had wanted to serve Him. She had given her life totally to God at the age of fifteen, spent a time at Cliff College, trained to be a nurse, and eventually married Trevor at the age of twenty-five. She had helped him as much as she could, being a mother, in his work in his churches, but she was not at all sure about the change from traditional, evangelical Anglicanism which had hit her husband and his new church. St Paul's was anything but traditional!

After a time, however, Anne realised that she too, like all those hundreds of people crowding into the church every Tuesday evening, and especially like Trevor, needed an infilling of spiritual power. She received the laying-on of hands for this blessing, and in a quiet moment was spiritually transformed into a very spiritually gifted woman.

We left St Paul's, Hainault, in 1975 to go out into all the world with our ministry. We lived "by faith", that is, without any certain income (or, at that time, a home to call our own) except what God's people felt led to give us. Anne actually began to lay hands on the sick on Trevor's discernment that this was God's will for her. Her healing ministry, alongside Trevor, began at a Methodist Church in Wisbech, Cambridgeshire, in 1975, whereupon sufferers began to experience healing from God through her ministry, as they have done ever since.

We have therefore been together "on the road" as itinerant evangelistic/healing ministers ever since we left St Paul's, Hainault. This itinerancy has had only a two-year lapse from 1981 to 1983 when Trevor was Rector at St Luke's Church, Seattle, USA, and interrupted by periods of enforced rest. God has blessed us with much prayer support and also love-gifts from His people in Britain, and we are very grateful to each one who has shared, and continues to share, in our ministry in this way.

In 1983 Trevor had a complete burn-out – an emotional and physical breakdown through tremendous overwork. God graciously raised him up again to a more modest ministry of healing after being retired by the Church of England, Episcopal Church of America and the Social Services. He has had to take long periods of rest, and Anne too has felt the physical and emotional cost of such an intensive ministry and also of looking after a burnt-out husband. However we still, at seventy years of age, serve the Lord and see His gracious blessing upon all we do in His name.

---

# *Part One*

---

## Miracles through
## the laying-on of hands

1

# 1

## God's use of hands in physical healing

### The healing of Ruth

Ruth was a small, single, former Salvation Army officer in her late sixties. She had been an officer in charge of several different Corps, and had served as a medical missionary in India. But serious illness forced her to leave full-time service. She was living on the Hainault estate and her interest in healing had come through books she had read on the subject. This is her story:

I had never been in a prayer meeting with such an awareness of the nearness of Jesus as on that Tuesday evening in St Paul's Hainault.

During the sermon given by Trevor Dearing I felt healing flowing into my body, bringing blood back to my limbs. I had been suffering from hardening of the arteries, resulting in extremely poor circulation, so that for some months I had rarely had any feeling in my hands and feet.. My foot and fingernails had turned black, and at times, especially during the night, I suffered excruciating pain, which not even eight hot water bottles resting on my feet and hands could relieve. I often paced the floor in sheer agony, not knowing how to cope with the pain.

I also suffered a severe thrombosis in one leg. I had felt that my days of health and service for Christ were over, until at this service I felt a tingling going through my limbs. When I later received the laying-on of hands, I went back to my seat, and to my delight I found that my hands were back to their normal colour and my legs and feet had new life. I felt waves of health sweeping through me. I was completely healed. My legs and feet were back to normal health, and I have never experienced any return of the symptoms. Praise God!

! ! ! ! ! ! ! ! ! ! ! ! ! ! ! ! ! ! ! ! ! ! ! ! ! ! ! ! ! ! ! ! ! ! ! ! ! ! ! ! !

*"These signs will accompany those who believe . . . they will place their hands on sick people, and they will get well."*

Such is the promise given to Christians in the traditional ending of Mark's gospel. Whatever one's views about the authenticity of these words (this ending being disputed by textual critics, as it is not included in the most ancient manuscripts) the use by God of the laying-on of hands to bring this grace, power and healing to the physically sick certainly dates back to the ministry of Jesus, who very frequently used this means of communicating the power of God to sick people

It also was most certainly used by the Apostles in "Acts", and all with wonderful miracles of healing taking place. It was therefore right and supernaturally natural that we should also use

3

this sacramental act in our ministry of healing, which Trevor did from the very beginning of his ministry at St Paul's, Hainault; and then we both did so in our joint itinerant ministry. God, our loving heavenly Father, deigned to use our ordinary human hands as a means by which He communicated His healing grace to the physically sick, to work miracles for them in their bodies.

# Dennis Houghton's testimony

*(A shortened version of this was added on the back cover of the paperback edition of* It's True!, *as it reached the publisher too late to be included in the book.)*

When I was twenty-three years of age I was a lorry roundsman, which was heavy work carrying 18-stone sacks of corn across farmyards, up steps and down narrow garden paths. I liked the outdoor life and I was also a keen sportsman, having a trial with Grimsby Town Football Club when Bill Shankley was the manager.

On one particular day I was carrying a sack of corn up into a barn, when the bag hit the top of the door and I lost control of it. In the process of trying to save it falling to the ground I felt something snap in my back, which left me in a semi-paralysed state. Later that same day I went to the doctor's, who took me off work and gave me some strong pain-killing tablets. I went back to work again after a few weeks, but I knew my days as a lorry driver were numbered. I later found a job as a milk roundsman, but after six months of continual pain things had gone from bad to worse. The hospital specialist told me that spondylitis had set in and that by the time I was forty I would be bent over. Finally, after three or four more changes of jobs doing lighter work and after having spells in hospital and many clinics, I was reaching the end of my tether.

My wife Joan was a keen Christian and had followed Trevor Dearing's ministry for a number of years. She believed that one day the Lord would heal me. By this time I was forty-three years of age and not able to get down to my feet. Joan had to help me with dressing. By now I could only manage to do office work, because I had difficulty standing, bending, kneeling and moving about.

At that time Trevor Dearing was holding monthly meetings at Stamford (60 miles away) and one Friday we arranged to take a coachload of people over to the meeting. When it came to the night I felt too tired to go, but Joan was persistent, so I went. We arrived at the meeting and participated in the worship and listening to the message, which was followed by ministry for healing.

By this time I felt too tired to move, but it was as though an invisible hand was pushing me forward. It was a cold night, but when Trevor prayed for me I felt a deep heat penetrate my body. I sank to the floor under the power of the Holy Spirit, and after some time I was helped to my feet. Very exhausted we went on our journey home. Joan helped me to bed as I was feeling completely shattered. It seemed like the end. I had tried everything but nothing had happened. Next morning, however, much to my great surprise I was able to dress myself and didn't need any more pain-killing tablets. The Lord had wonderfully healed me. I found I could now run up the office steps, and play football, cricket and tennis with my teenage boys.

I am now sixty-one years old and although I have to take some medication each night I have been able to continue to go to work until last year when I took early retirement. Besides this I have been able to serve on the local Town Council for many years, two of them as Chairman.

[*And a more recent note:*] I'll be 70 next year, and am still playing tennis, doing D.I.Y. and gardening. My back is better than new.

!!!!!!!!!!!!!!!!!!!!!!!!!!!!!!!!!!!!!!!!!!!!!!!!!!!

# Beryl

A vicar from the Midlands sent us the following after one of our meetings

A parishioner, Beryl, was due to go into hospital for a second mastectomy, and also a lump had developed under her armpit. When she attended the meeting she was very fearful, and only half hopeful when you laid your hands upon her and prayed for her.

Afterwards she was examined by the doctor prior to the operation. "It appears to be dissolving," he commented incredulously, "but whatever you do, come back in a month for further examination."

A month later doctors were unable to find any trace of cancer in her body. They are completely mystified as to what has happened to bring about this change in her condition. But Beryl knows! She cannot stop praising the Lord for His mercy and is praying for greater boldness in testifying to others of the healing power of Christ.

✤ ✤ ✤ ✤ ✤ ✤ ✤ ✤ ✤ ✤ ✤ ✤ ✤ ✤ ✤ ✤ ✤ ✤ ✤ ✤ ✤ ✤ ✤ ✤ ✤

# From a lady in Stourbridge, West Midlands

**1992**

I don't know whether you will remember us from the Hodge Hill Methodist Church on Sunday November 27th at 10.30 a.m. My husband and I came up together and asked you to pray for a man called Sam who was in hospital. Two years ago he had had **both his kidneys out**. You prayed for him then and he recovered. Well he seems to be on the mend again as he came out of hospital one week later, although his treatment is ongoing for 3 months. — Miracle number one.

6

Then my husband asked you to pray for me because I was suffering from spondylitis in my neck, and you said, "Spondylitis go!!" and it did. I could not believe it at first, that it had happened to me, that THE LORD had touched me through you, but the second miracle had taken place, and now I can walk, drive, swim, iron, hoover and hold my head up without pain. I do not have to lie on the floor for hours to give the muscles in my neck a rest, just to do normal housework.

# Another from the West Midlands:
## Ruth Zingers, from Walsall:

Just to let you know that since the prayer (at Hockley) for my neck and shoulder I have had painless nights. After a fall in Israel I had continuous pain in my right shoulder, and had treatment with physiotherapy and drugs to no avail. Having had arthritis in my neck for many years, which was healed through prayer in 1964, the fall aggravated it. But I have had great relief since that night in Hockley. Praise Jesus our LORD.

P.S. Also blood pressure healed.

Mary, Whitefield

"Dear Anne,

"When you and Trevor came to Little Lever Christian Fellowship to speak and minister healing to us, I brought a neighbour named Mary to the Saturday evening meeting who had just been told she had cancer. She went forward for healing and you laid hands on her and prayed that God would heal her.

"Only 3 weeks before this she had a hysterectomy, and it was then that the cancer was found. She was quite weak afterwards, but on that evening God spoke to her and told her to come to the meeting. She had always read her Bible and prayed, but never went to church until a year before.

7

"I gave her Colin Urquhart's book Listen and Live, and she began to read it. She was told she had to have 6 monthly treatments of chemo-therapy and after the first one I went to see her and to pray with her. I was amazed at the change in her. She was so positive – quoting all the texts about healing, and applying them to herself.

"After the first treatment she was sick for a fortnight and could not eat or drink much. When she was at her lowest physically and crying out to the Lord for His help, He spoke to her one night to get out of bed, walk about and sing praises – which she did. Then He said, "You have not chosen Me, but I have chosen you", and then He flooded her with His joy.

"A few weeks later, when the continual sickness was very hard to bear, and I was praying with her, a similar thing happened, and even though very weak, she jumped up and sang praises to the Lord in a very strong voice. Again He filled her with His joy, and met her need again in the only way that could work for her. I was so thrilled at the way in which Jesus met her need in such a personal and definite way, and I blessed and thanked Him, for often I felt incapable of helping her at these difficult times.

"You may be wondering why I am giving you all these details, but last week she had to go to the hospital for the results of the scan – this was last Thursday – and she was then told that she was clear of the cancer. Ever since you prayed for her she has believed that God was healing her. She was always thanking Him for this, and He has been faithful, as He promised."

# At St Mary's Church, Eastham 2001
## Mrs D. B. tells her story:

Dear Reverend Dearing,
. . . I had gone to that particular service in that church on that evening because it was a United Service and I had absolutely no prior knowledge that you were taking it or that it was to be a Healing Service . . .

In 2000 I had been diagnosed as having cancer of the womb. I must say, wisely or not, I did not follow the normal operation/chemotherapy route, as I wanted to find a natural cure, which I believed at that time that I had done. The only thing was that I had been left with what I described best as "cranky" hands. They were very swollen and difficult to bend, and I had decided that I had to learn to live with them.

When you invited people to come and receive healing from you I decided to see if anything could be done for my hands. The first few people who had received healing had, to my amazement, all fallen to the floor. When I did not fall to the floor I assumed that it must not have worked for me. I wasn't in any way critical. I just appreciated that, just as in the medical world with the best will in the world, not all cures work for all people.

I returned to my pew and sat down, and to my amazement the inside of my head started vibrating very strongly indeed, and for some considerable time it felt as though all the ions in it were moving forwards and backwards very straight and very rapidly. It didn't hurt at all. My former minister of St John's C. of E. church in Guilden Sutton, the Rev. John Malbon, described it as though the Holy Ghost had entered me, when I told him about it.

When it finally stopped I noticed that my hands were completely back to normal and that I could move them as flexibly as ever I could. I was thrilled and when I came to buy

9

your book from you I said, "It worked. It worked." Canon Winstanley, who was standing in close proximity to us, said in an amused voice, "That's what it is supposed to do", which made me smile. It was because I had not fallen over on your laying-on of hands on me that I thought that it hadn't worked.

Even better, I had visited my doctor on the Saturday morning before the church service on the Sunday evening with very painful heels. She said that I had some very nasty blisters and that I should come and see the District Nurse at the surgery early on Monday morning to have them attended to, which I did. The District Nurse looked at my heels and said there was nothing there. They had definitely been there when I had gone to church the evening before, as I was wearing special boots which did not rub them, although after the church service I had been so delighted with my hands returning to normal, which is all that I had asked for, I had not given any thought to my heels.

The final miracle was to my legs. I had retired from 35 years as a Secondary age PE specialist in 1996. My legs had given me real problems in my final few weeks. I felt that I could barely put one foot in front of the other, the result, I deduced, of being on my feet and on the go for 35 years. It seemed as though my leg muscles had lost their elasticity. It really spoilt the early years of my retirement. Lo and behold, a day after your healing my legs were fine. Cynics told me that none of the healing would last. Well it has lasted up to now and I have no reason to believe that it will change. My hands, heels and legs are all functioning perfectly normally and I am truly very grateful indeed to you. Thank you very much.

(Dated 26 March 2003.)

# "The worst back he had ever seen"

"As I said to you, you healed my back many years ago after I had been through a lot of agony.

"I had had treatment at St Thomas' Hospital, lumbar puncture in Bow from Dr Syriac, and had been in the Royal Homeopathic Hospital under Mr Churchill-Davidson, who said mine was the worst back he had ever seen. All to no avail.

"We were living in Battersea at the time, and a friend phoned to say what a wonderful healing you had done for a friend of hers. She said, 'Unfortunately he is in Hainault, and you would never make it there. However, Nicholas Rivet-Corrnack has a healing service at the Holy Trinity, perhaps you could get there'"

"I phoned Nicholas, and he said, 'Oh! Do come along. It's going to be a great service because, for the first time, Trevor Dearing will be here.'

"I had to hold the roof of the car in order to enter the car. I drove to the Holy Trinity, received my healing, almost ran back to the car, and have never had any trouble with my back since."

**James St. George-Kennedy**

*To God be the glory!*

# Val King's story

It was three weeks before Christmas. I was at college, working hard on my Christmas cake, which meant bending over a lot. When I had finished, I sat up, feeling quite pleased with my cake, when suddenly, I felt this hot sensation across my back. I thought it would go away. Then my neck went stiff and I couldn't turn my head, so I made an appointment to see my doctor. He said it would go away and gave me some medication to help with the inflammation.

About a week later I experienced a severe pain in my head, neck and right shoulder and arm. I thought I'd had a stroke. At the hospital I sat in the waiting room for three hours, in constant pain. When I was seen by the doctor, he told me that I had trapped nerves in my back. He gave me strong pain killers and sleeping tablets.

My parents looked after me over the Christmas holidays. It was then that the anxiety set in and I felt my whole world was falling apart. A strong sense of fear overwhelmed me. I began to experience rapid heart beats, feeling shaky, breathing problems, pins and needles in my hands, and a fear of going out. To get myself through this, I would sing hymns and read scripture, especially Psalm 62, verses 1 and 2.

One morning while I was making myself a cup of tea, a package arrived from UCB. As I read it, it was as if God was sitting next to me. He told me to put my college course on hold because it would not be fruitful at this time and that I needed to come close to Him to gain new strength. I spent time with God each morning. He told me that if I carried on with college, my injuries would be a lot worse. So I left college and put everything into God's hands.

As the days went by, I was so close to God, I could almost touch Him. His presence was so strong. It was then that my anxiety lessened and it was replaced by peace. God said to me: **"Val, don't give up, I will restore you and give you the grace to get back on your feet again,"**

When I saw a physiotherapist, I discovered that I had a slipped disc in the neck and not trapped nerves in my back! It was such a relief to know what was wrong with me. I was still in a lot of pain, but God told me to stay focused on Him.

On February 22nd, 1998 the pain was so bad that I cried most of the morning. I got on my knees and asked God to help me because I couldn't stand the pain any longer. I picked up my Bible and began to read it. God said to me:

**"You are not alone today, I feel your pain and I know your heartache. I will help you today."**

Later that day Brenda rang me. She told me about the Trevor Dearing service which had been held on the Saturday. Then she asked me how I felt. I explained that I was not so good, that the pain was really bad. Brenda asked:

"Would you like me to get in touch with Trevor and see if he will pray with you tonight, before the service, then I will bring you straight home?"

I said, "OK."

Brenda rang me back and said, "You're not going to believe this. Trevor said, 'Tell Val to come ten minutes before the service, and tell her she will stay for the rest of the service!' "

I thought, you're joking, I can't even sit in a chair!

I arrived at Church at about 6.20 pm. As I walked into the vestry, my eyes met with Trevor's. He seemed to glow, and a sense of peace filled the air. Trevor asked me what was wrong, so I explained. He said, "Why be in pain when Jesus is here. You have been in pain too long."

A small group was gathering and my son was present. Trevor placed his hand on my head and prayed over me. I was filled with the anointing of the Holy Spirit and went over onto the floor. God spoke through Trevor, that He loved me, and wanted me to have true peace and happiness. AND just as Trevor had said, I stayed for the rest of the service! I witnessed so many blessings, it was a real privilege to be there.

The next day I woke up with no pain. Although I was still stiff and sore, my pain had gone, and I believe that I was healed of my pain by God, through Trevor Dearing.

## Miracles of healing at meetings of the
# Full Gospel Businessmen's Fellowship International

There have been many instances of healing at these meetings where we have ministered in the name of Jesus. The following is the latest testimony we have received:

## Shirley, Deganwy 2003

"I will praise <u>YOU</u>, O Lord, with all my heart. I will tell of <u>YOUR</u> wonders. I will be glad and rejoice in <u>YOU</u>; I will sing praise to your name, O Most High."

(Psalm 9 v 1-2)

11th October 2003

Dear Mr Dearing,

My husband and I joined the Full Gospel Business Men at Beechwood Court, Conwy, on 2 September . . . but only to hear your testimony and then, for the beginning of your healing ministry. We came for only part of the evening because I had been diagnosed as having cancer of the oesophagus earlier the same day . . . so I was physically and emotionally drained. You prayed for me personally.

Between 2 Sept and 16 Sept God healed me of this cancer. A specialist from Bangor Hospital saw my husband and me to <u>show</u> us the results on 3 October, of a second endoscopy and biopsies, which he took on 16 September. The result? Whereas "a nodule of cancer cells" showed on the original photograph, there was no sign of cancer on the photograph of the second endoscopy and biopsies. None at all!

We praise God from the bottom of our hearts and thank both you, and all those who prayed for us, for being instrumental in this wonderful healing.

Yours sincerely, in our Lord Jesus,

S. B.

# Heather's story 2002

Just over 12 years ago I started to feel very tired. This was not normal tiredness, it was unremitting, like a heavy weight pressing down on me all the time. It never eased up, however much rest I had. My legs were aching constantly, like cramp. I was constantly having to fight off depression, and worst of all, I found it very difficult to sleep at night, which just made everything worse.

After some visits to the doctor, I was eventually diagnosed as having M.E. Many friends prayed for me, and although I responded to calls for prayer at various Christian meetings over the years, this made no difference.

However, I was sure that Jesus would heal me, and even from those early years, my husband Clive and I used to thank Jesus in our prayers every night for the healing that we had asked of Him.

Life has to go on, and over the years I found I could cope by rising in the morning after 9.30 am, and then having a rest all

15

afternoon. So my life was restricted to just a few hours a day: the morning, and from early evening until around 10.00 pm. However, it was impossible to do anything active, and if I did stay up during the afternoon for a few days, it used to take me weeks to recover.

Every few years I did return to the doctor for more tests, to check that nothing else was causing the symptoms, and even tried some of the drug treatments, but it made no difference.

Clive was asked by the Full Gospel Businessmen's Fellowship International Directors to be involved in arranging the National Convention to be at Llandudno this year, and I decided I was going to attend. It was close to home, so I did not have any tiring travelling to do or accommodation to arrange. The highlight for me was on Sunday morning, when Trevor Dearing was ministering.

He was sharing how we needed to commit our whole lives to Jesus Christ, and asked us to sing together "When I survey the wondrous cross". As I did this, and got onto my knees, I suddenly felt that weight that had come upon me all those years ago completely lift away.

I turned to Clive who was next to me and told him, "It's gone!" I knew I had been completely healed. Trevor asked for those who required healing to come into the aisles of the hall to have the Directors lay hands on them as Trevor prayed, and I did this as an acknowledgement of what had happened.

Since that moment, I feel like I did those 12 years ago before it came. I am having to take things carefully because my muscles need to build up again. But I am now working in the garden and on our smallholding, doing jobs I have not even been able to contemplate for the last 12 years. I have been able to accompany Clive doing things together again, just like we used to. I still get tired when I do too much, but it is a natural tiredness, that is balanced by natural rest. The oppression, heaviness and all the other symptoms of M.E. have gone forever.

I just want to thank Jesus, and give all the glory to Him. He DOES answer our prayers, as we continually hold fast to His promises, and thank Him for what He has done.

# At a meeting of FGBMFI, Norwich

Here a lady gave testimony recently to the way in which the Lord used Anne to heal her of cancer within four days. She also told how her son had been born with twisted feet, about which the surgeons could do very little. After Anne ministered to him 20 years ago his feet straightened. He is now an athlete and wins all his sprint races at College.

## At Stamford FGBMFI

A lady who had been bedridden and hadn't been able to bend down for 20 years was healed after Trevor had laid hands on her in the name of Jesus. Now she can touch her toes.

# The healing of Graham Cavanagh at a meeting of FGBMFI
*This is his story:*

It was early December 1997. I was clearing away the leaves from the driveway when suddenly a severe pain struck my chest — something I never experienced before! Afterwards, the pains would return every time I exerted myself or whenever I was anxious or got worked up about something. I hoped this was a temporary thing and that it would go away. Instead it got worse.

The doctor sent me for a stress test to discover if I had a heart problem. On the day of the test, I went on a treadmill and was expected to walk briskly for about ten minutes. I never managed it, the doctor switching the machine off after only two minutes. The results showed I had severe angina and would have to take pills to control the problem.

At the hospital, I had an angiogram, where a series of pictures of all the arteries inside my heart were taken to find out what surgery was needed. They discovered that three of my arteries were narrow, restricting the flow of blood. I would need a **triple by-pass operation**! I was placed on the waiting list and told I would have to wait from nine to twelve months. During this waiting time I grew progressively worse and had to stop work. I didn't want to do this as I was self-employed, but it was **impossible** to carry on — I felt so ill.

All through this time, being a Christian, I hoped Jesus would heal me and save me from having to go through with the heart surgery, and with this in mind *took every opportunity* to be prayed for to be healed. On December 7th 1998 (a year to the day since I first started with pains) I went to a Full Gospel Businessmen's Meeting, where Christians have a meal and get to hear a testimony, and also have the opportunity to be prayed for. I received the laying-on of hands for healing [Trevor's ministry] and from that day I began to feel increasingly better. I stopped all the pills and never looked back!

I **knew** Jesus had healed me and went back to work without any problems! I also decided to go back to the doctor to tell him what had happened. Well, of course he had a problem understanding what had happened! When I told him I'd stopped taking my pills he immediately took my blood pressure and cholesterol level. They were quite high before, but now were **normal**! He urged me to go back to hospital for a check-up.

The surgeon there was quite upset that I'd stopped my pills and told me to start taking them again because I was putting

18

myself at risk. I told him I was now well and didn't need the surgery. He replied *this was impossible* and that I would be advised to have the operation when it became due. I asked him if I could have more tests to confirm I was well, but was refused because the results would be "just the same".

There seemed to be only one avenue left open to me, and that was to take a further angiogram privately. When I saw the heart consultant I explained to him that as a Christian I believed that Jesus had healed me. I told him I had been to meetings where I had seen the blind receive their sight, the deaf receive their hearing, and people who couldn't walk get out of their wheelchairs! After hearing what I had to say he agreed that further tests would certainly prove one way or the other what, if anything, had happened.

A week later I was admitted to hospital and had the angiogram. When the consultant saw me later he explained that the three narrowed arteries were just the same — *but that something else had happened*. The heart has two main arteries to it which supply the blood: my left was normal, but the right one had become extremely large, *twice the width it originally was*. In his own words, he explained that my heart in effect now had a by-pass and that the enlarged artery was now more than adequate to supply extra blood to my heart. A few days later he then gave me another stress test just to make sure my heart was back to normal. I sailed through it, doing the full ten minutes with no problems whatsoever! In fact the consultant complimented me saying my heart now had a very good pumping action!

The consultant wrote to the heart surgeon at the hospital, explaining his findings, and he arranged for me to see him. He agreed there was now no reason to have the heart surgery — which I was very pleased about!

In closing let me say that I will always be grateful to Jesus for what He did for me; He healed me and saved me from surgery. I cannot thank Him enough. And yes, He's *still* working miracles in people's lives today, just as He did when He walked the earth about 2000 years ago! To God be the Glory!

# Eddie, Bolton

"You were speaking at our FGBMFI meeting in Bolton on the 7th December 1998, and Jim brought you to our house, where I was ill in bed. The doctor had been that day and told us that things weren't very good and that my lungs were **being eaten away**.

"You came that night and prayed over me with the laying-on of hands, and that night I began to feel better, and the Lord told me He was going to do a mighty work. After being in bed 7 weeks I was up the following day, and praise God, every day. I no longer need oxygen after using it most days, and I have been able to cut down the use of my nebuliser from 8 times a day to (at the time of writing) 3 or 4 times.

"Thank you Trevor for your faithfulness to the Lord and for your ministry to me that night. We give Jesus all the praise and all the glory, trusting He will continue to use you in His service."

# Leyton, London E10
# Ina Maud Redmond's story

1996. I had had awful migraine for forty-four years, and was almost blind. The left eye was sightless and the right almost so. When I was brought to Hainault that evening I went down to Trevor and told him in a few words what was wrong.

I did not hear him pray. He laid his hands on me and I was "slain in the Spirit". I was lifted up and went back to my seat, still in a lot of pain. But during the night God healed me. I have never had a headache since.

My eyes were also healed. I am only able to write to you as my sight was restored that night, on 20th November 1972.

Our God is so wonderful.

# An unusual testimony

*On one occasion some years ago Anne asked Trevor to accompany her to a dress shop in Stamford, where they live, to see if he liked a skirt and blouse that she had tried on.*

*Trevor remembers:* While she was going through the process of putting the clothes on, I noticed that one of the two assistants was looking at me with a puzzled expression on her face.

I agreed that the clothes looked very nice on Anne, and decided to pay by credit card. Of course, my name was on the card and at the sight of it, the assistant's expression completely changed.

*"That's* who you are!" she said excitedly. "Now I know where I've seen you. But you look different from that time when you were younger and had long hair."

She went on to explain: "I was once very ill and crippled up with arthritis at a young age. I really had no future. Then I saw your healing ministry on television. I found out where your next meeting was taking place and followed you around all over the country, my husband driving me everywhere. The very first time you ever laid hands on me, I found myself falling backwards, and was completely healed. I now live in one of the villages outside Stamford and come in to work here. Fancy meeting up with you again after the passing of all these years!"

21

This testimony certainly made our day, and whenever Anne wears her outfit I remember yet another person, previously unknown to us, whom God was pleased to help and heal through the ministry He so graciously has given to us.

# Ingatestone, Essex
# Mrs Joyce Cowan's testimony

A terrible car accident left me paralysed from the neck down. My spinal and vocal cords were damaged and my bladder injured. They told me I'd have to wear a drainage tube for the rest of my life. But after prayer with the laying- on of hands by Trevor Dearing, I've made a wonderful recovery and no longer need it.

Mrs Cowan's GP, Dr David Frampton, confirmed this. He said, "There was a dramatic change in her condition after she saw Rev. Dearing. She can now walk unaided and her internal injuries — which medical treatment could not help further — are now cured."

\* \* \* \* \* \* \* \* \* \* \* \* \* \* \* \* \* \* \* \* \* \* \* \* \* \* \* \* \* \* \* \* \*

Trevor has had all sorts of strange but pleasant surprises at meetings. One lady insisted on walking up to the front of the church carrying what, from a distance, looked like a huge piece of medieval armour. It turned out to be a medical saddle-leather jacket weighing nine pounds. The lady had brought it to give thanks to God that she no longer needed to wear it to support what had been a crumbling spine. How the congregation praised the Lord!

Another demonstration at a meeting was when a man who had been unable to walk properly began to tap dance on the church floor. Later he wrapped the crepe bandage with which his leg had been supported around the walking stick which had borne his weight, and laid them on the altar in thanksgiving.

This laying down of walking sticks became quite a feature of Trevor's meetings. There was

## Brian

who *had never walked more than a few steps*, but after prayer, in the sight of everyone, actually walked the length of the Guildhall steps and out to a car on his own.

# A baby who was born blind

One of the most memorable cases of healing that Trevor remembers was the child of Salvation Army parents. The baby girl had been born blind. He recalls:

They brought her to St Paul's on a Tuesday evening and I laid hands on the baby's eyes.

"Let there be sight, Lord," I prayed. I went on: "Jesus, who healed the eyes of the blind Bartimaeus, heal this child's eyes now."

On the following Thursday the baby had another appointment at Moorfield's Eye Hospital which was caring for her. The parents telephoned the vicarage excitedly on Thursday afternoon.

"There's been a miracle!" they exclaimed. **"Irises which were non-existent** in our baby's eyes have actually appeared and grown, and the glaucoma has subsided. They say she can see!"

The last contact we had with that family was when the parents sent us a photograph of their daughter some years later, actually riding a bicycle down the road.

!!!!!!!!!!!!!!!!!!!!!!!!!!!!!!!!!!!!!!!!!!!!!!!!!!!!

# Hearing restored

Deafness as well as blindness, was healed by the Lord at St Paul's, Hainault. One of the most moving cases was that of a country vicar in Essex, who loved to listen to classical music, but because of his deafness was deprived of this pleasure. Trevor prayed for him and he wrote afterwards to say, "I can now hear even the faintest sounds of individual instruments in the orchestra!"

# Elizabeth and cerebral palsy

Seemingly, she had no future, for Elizabeth was a little girl afflicted with cerebral palsy. But after Trevor had prayed for her with the laying-on of hands, her parents wrote:

> It is with great joy and thankfulness that we write to tell you of Elizabeth's progress. She is now talking so much, that we sometimes have to tell her to be quiet. Three years ago we were told that she would never speak, or in fact do anything at all.
>
> **She is now at school (full time) and is learning to read and write and do all the normal things that children do. It is wonderful to hear her singing carols and taking part in a nativity play. How good the Lord has been to us!**

# Epilepsy healed

Epilepsy is a terrible affliction. Sufferers go through untold mental agony, not knowing when they will have their next attack, and many are unemployable for this reason. One such epileptic was Trevor from Ilford who, after being healed for over three years, could not find employment because employers just couldn't believe he was healed after being so ill.

He told his story to the Southend Echo:

> I first started having epileptic fits when I was 12, and was having 3 a day when I came to St Paul's. I didn't have any faith until I experienced the atmosphere and the way of worship here. It was a wonderful experience and relieved me of anxiety about my condition. I believe faith has completely stopped my attacks.

# Southport

*Anne remembers a Methodist Holiness Convention:*

I came in at the tent door, and I was walking past a great many chairs, and sat next to a lady who was sitting alone. She was *amazed* that I should sit next to her, as she told me later in a letter. She told me about her terrible migraine headaches; how she had seen various physicians and specialists, and spent periods of time in hospital in attempts to remedy them. But they just could not be cured. She had to stay in darkened rooms day in and day out, the pain was so intense.

So I ministered to her. I just laid my hands on her head as she was sitting there, and I said, "Lord, take these headaches away once and for all." She wrote to me some months later

25

from Sheffield, identifying herself as the woman in the tent, and saying that God had healed her completely; she had no more bad heads. She wrote again several years later, to say there had been no recurrence of those dreadful pains.

# J. G.F., York

"It was under your ministry in York on November 21st 1980 that I was healed. It was in fact your wife who actually prayed for me. Not only was I healed of severe degenerative arthritis of the spine, but also an intense abdominal pain (undiagnosed) went too.

"A half-hearted, backslidden Christian at the time, during the moments that I lay on the floor under God's power my whole heart did an 'about turn' to God, so that from then on I have known a commitment to Him and to His purposes I had never before experienced. I think, during that time He must have 'baptised' me in His love, because up to then I never could love Him properly — didn't know how to — and so couldn't serve Him in obedience as I wanted, though I had in fact been a Christian since 1962.

"It hasn't all been roses since. There have been difficulties, but it has been a time of growth and strengthening, of learning to trust God and how He has set me in the way He wants me to go.

"I was heavily addicted to prescribed drugs and alcohol before that night in 1980 and now feel very much I want to help others in like state. I came right off all drugs at that time, and though I went through a terrible withdrawal in the following days and weeks, God's presence and strength was enough to keep me. I'm glad I didn't miss out the withdrawal, because I feel I got to know God better during those dark days and also gained an understanding into the mental suffering that many go through (for all sorts of reasons). It's good to understand how

26

people feel when you pray for them — it helps one to pray more effectively.

"One big thank you to both of you for letting God use you to change my whole life."

## John, Bents Green Methodist Church

Two or three years ago you came to speak at Bents Green Methodist Church here. Our son John, 15, went forward for prayer [with the laying-on of hands], and came back looking just the same – (a bad heart case, expected to die before 3 when we adopted him as a baby, having had quite a few "holding operations" performed by the Lord, but still basically blue and unable to hold his own with his peers) – the next day though, we knew something wonderful had happened.

We all went on a Bank Holiday church ramble, and we always had to carry John every 5 minutes, which meant arriving back with him half an hour after everyone else. This time **he started off first, and arrived back first**, with no help at all!

And when he went for the "very serious, maybe fatal" heart operation a few months later, the consultant himself wheeled John back from the operating theatre half an hour later. He said that he'd never seen anything like it, the Almighty must have got there first.

So a thousand million thanks for all your obedience to the Lord, and may He continue to bless you mightily.

## Mrs G.O., Staffordshire

"This is my testimony — About 8 years ago you held a Supper and Healing service just before Christmas. I came with my niece — she was born autistic; she could not read or write; she needed 24-hourly supervision because she also had epileptic fits.

All she could do with her life was to go to a Daily Centre for backward people.

"I was determined she would not spend the rest of her life like this. So in faith I brought her up to you for a blessing. For the past seven years her life has changed, and now she holds down a job at Sainsburys Supermarket. She travels there, can shop, go to the dentist and doctor's all on her own, go to the hairdressers, do any normal thing. So you see, Rev Dearing, my niece was completely healed. Thank you sir, and praise the Lord."

# Wendy, Minsteracres

"For at least 7 years I had pain in the lower back, and especially after sitting, when it took time to straighten up from a bent-over position. X-rays showed osteo-arthritis. The G.P. supplied me with large boxes of Co-codamol and advised me to lie flat as much as possible rather than sitting.

"Since you prayed for me on the Friday evening Anne, and I rested in the Spirit during the first session, the pain has gone. Even after sitting I can stand upright, praise the Lord. You also prayed for special blessings over the weekend — and there were many!

"On the Sunday afternoon you prayed for me, Trevor, when I asked for a refilling of the Holy Spirit and healing in our family. I have been experiencing wonderful answers to this prayer since then.

"Thanks so much for all you shared of yourselves and God's miracles — to send us out renewed in faith and expectancy."

# Pauline

"In December 1998 we brought Pauline, who was pronounced terminally ill with a brain tumour, to see you. [In August she almost died.] Well – you should see her now! She made steady progress from that time and has become a radiant woman. The hospital recently said, 'Come for a check-up in a year's time.' They don't want to X-ray her – they believe that there is no threat to her life any more.

Praise God for all His goodness!"

*Pauline herself writes:*

"To lose my driving licence (because of the seizures) was a devastating blow. I had driven a vehicle virtually every day since I was 18 years old. At one time I had a thoroughly enjoyable driving job, which took me all around parts of Essex, Suffolk and Norfolk. Having no licence meant I could not carry on with my photography business, as I was unable to get to my clients; playgroups, schools, etc.

"When I saw my consultant in May 2001 she suggested I began making enquiries as to the possibility of applying for my driving licence. I could hardly believe my ears! After filling in all the necessary forms, and the DVLA obtaining the medical reports they needed, I regained my licence on 27th November, 2001. What a wonderful day and most of all, what a wonderful God."

# The healing of Becky
# St John's Church, Westwood, Coventry

*This is her testimony, after Anne's ministry:*

Last summer I went to India for five weeks with a team project that was run by Tear Fund. We were working in schools in the heart of the slums of Calcutta. It was the most amazing experience of my life. It was absolutely fantastic.

But within three days of arriving there I became ill, with continual vomiting. I couldn't keep anything down. The team prayed for me, so I was able to keep going, but I still couldn't keep anything down. I was given a word from the Lord: "My grace is sufficient for you; for My power is made perfect in weakness".

I was excited when I got home. I thought, 'I'll soon be back to normal and back at University.' But the illness continued. It just got worse. But God helped me through it. He gave me the strength for each day. The doctors at home couldn't do anything. They sent me to the tropical diseases clinic in London, but they couldn't do anything.

I went back to University, but I was no better. It got worse and worse. So just before Christmas I ended up in hospital. I had no nutrition in me whatsoever. The doctors had no idea what to do. At one point I had eight doctors round my bed. And they thought if they were to rehydrate me I would be better. So they put me on a drip for a week and sent me home. But I was no better

I got through the second term, but it was really tough, and God taught me a lot about relying on Him. I kept taking that verse, as He helped me through each day.

The third term I was to do teaching practice, and I was even worse physically. I got less and less sleep. It was just a nightmare. The only thing I could eat was white bread. On the Sundays when I was doing Sunday School in the morning I usually went to the evening service. This particular Sunday I felt so ill and tired, I decided that I would *not* be going in the evening. Then I heard Peter saying that the evening service would be a healing service. All through the morning I felt that I wanted to go, but I thought, 'No, I'm too tired. I really don't want to go.'

I was really ill all afternoon, but I thought, 'I'm not going to let this opportunity slip away from me'. So I grabbed a carrier bag and just ran to get on the bus, and when I got to the church I had to go straight to the toilet with sickness yet again.

I can't remember the name of the guy who was taking the healing service. He was saying, "If you *really* want to get better, God will heal you." And I remember feeling cross, thinking, 'Do you really think I don't want to get better?!'

I stood in the queue of people waiting to be prayed for, then the man's wife prayed for me with the laying-on of hands. The moment she did so, I felt a warmth going through my body down to my stomach.. And I realised that the pain had stopped. I was not hurting for the first time in nine months. I was amazed. I hadn't been expecting anything to happen. It was absolutely amazing. I'd forgotten what it felt like to be normal. I felt warm, and at peace.

As I sat there listening to the guy speaking, I did feel that God was speaking to me, because I had been scared, through those months, that if I was healed I wouldn't be able to do all the things that had become a problem — that I would never feel 100%.

That evening I was under a kind of attack, and also during the following week. I heard a little voice inside saying "Be careful, only try a little bit of something . . .", but I said, "*No!* I'm going to have my first really good meal!" So I cooked myself a massive meal, with no ill effects. Then at breakfast next morning there was this little voice tempting me to be cautious, saying, "You'd better not have much, and just a little soya milk . . ." But I said, "*No!* I'm going to have a really big bowl of cereal, with loads and loads of milk!"

31

I haven't had any problems since. There's nothing I can't eat now. I just feel so grateful. It's amazing to be feeling 100% again!

# A memorable miracle in Finland

Anne remembers:

Perhaps the most momentous miracle in my own ministry occurred when Trevor and I were missioning in Finland. How those Finnish people packed into the churches! I remember one night when hundreds stood outside the church because it was packed to capacity. They waited patiently outside until Trevor had finished his message, but all began to crowd round us as soon as they knew that the healing ministry had begun. Trevor and I were pressed back almost to the walls of the church, and were laying hands on people who were falling to the floor under the power of the Holy Spirit the moment we touched them.

It was difficult to grasp what was happening at the time, especially when one lady got up from the floor and began shouting excitedly in Finnish and running around the church. It was months later that we received a copy of a Finnish Christian periodical in which it was recounted that this woman, previously totally blind, *with the retinas of her eyes destroyed*, had received her sight! Glory be to Jesus!

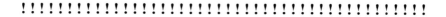

All this shows that God is interested in our *physical* as well as our spiritual well-being, and that "His touch has still its ancient power."

These are only a few of the hundreds of first-hand testimonies we have received, testifying that Jesus is healing the sick today through the laying-on of hands. We would emphasise that this is not a matter of a magical healing touch. Healing flows through a deep encounter and involvement with Jesus, as a person. It comes through a relationship with Him based on deep trust in His promises. We would — much like Peter in Acts Chapter 3, verses 11 and 16 — say to people: "Do not look at us as if through our own power or holiness we had made this man walk. It is by His name, through faith in His name, that these people have been given this perfect soundness in the presence of you all."

# 2

## *God's use of human hands in healing of the mind and emotions*

In our ministry we not only saw God healing the physically sick through the laying-on of hands, but also the emotionally ill. These included sufferers from chronic, acute depression, phobias, and panic attacks, and even the psychologically ill. It seems that as we laid our hands upon these sufferers that the Holy Spirit reached deep down into the recesses of their minds, healing rejection, hurts, traumas, painful memories — even those which had been consciously forgotten — in fact God brought His miraculous healing balm into the patient's entire being. Again, these miracles took place at St Paul's, Hainault, and widely in our itinerant ministry.

# Carol

She was only twenty-four years old, but after a shattering breakdown looked more like a woman of forty, and lived on a life-line of anti-depressant drugs.

Her battle for sanity ended when Trevor prayed for her at the church. She told her story to a local newspaper in 1974:

"My marriage broke up nearly three years ago and I took it very badly. I spent some time in a psychiatric hospital. I returned home dependent on anti-depressant tablets and sleeping pills.

"I used to hide in my room and chain smoke all day. My mother told Mr Dearing about the state I was in and he persuaded me to come along.

"I can't remember doing it, but I went forward. Mr Dearing laid hands on me and prayed for me.

"When I walked out of the church I found the nearest drain and threw my tablets down it. I realised God loved me and had healed me."

Carol's healing was so thorough that a few years later she qualified as a nurse in a psychiatric hospital, caring for people suffering as she once did. A little later she was voted Nurse of the Year at her hospital. Such was the complete healing God gave her.

Carol wrote to us a couple of years ago:

"I have felt for a long time that I should write to you and thank you for all you have done in my life — bringing me into the fullness of Christ through His Spirit. Thank you for your teaching and encouragement.

"Well, 26½ years on, Ian pastors the local Elim Church, we have two now grown-up children: our daughter is 22 and our son is a fine godly young man of 20 who has just returned from Canada after being in School of Ministry, then working as a musician with an evangelist.

"I'm still nursing part time in an E.M.I. (Elderly Mentally Ill) unit. So much has happened in all these years and I know much of your influence has been a great input into our lives. So thank you Trevor and Anne and God bless you as you bless others."

# Marcia, the clergyman's wife

She was a slim-built, pretty mother of four children, the wife of a Christian minister. When her fourth child was born she suddenly became deeply depressed — a depression that got darker and blacker each day.

When Marcia first came to our Tuesday evening meeting she was suffering such intense depression that she sobbed through the first two hours of the meeting. She was due to see her psychiatrist next day, and knew that, humanly speaking, a fourth admittance into a mental hospital was inevitable.

Her illness was so acute that she had to take massive doses of tranquillisers and sedatives, but life was still intolerable. The drugs hardly blocked out the horrifying nothingness of her life.

Marcia was too distressed to move out of her pew to receive ministry, so Trevor laid hands on her as she sat in the choir stalls. After this prayer she became more peaceful and came forward to receive anointing with oil.

Anne then took her into a vestry for counselling, and she emerged a transformed woman. She had known and loved Jesus as her Saviour for many years, but now she knew Him as her healer and baptiser in the Holy Spirit.

She told us later that the psychiatrist was amazed at the remarkable change, because she was now filled with joy and happiness. She was immediately able to manage without her tablets. A month later the psychiatrist saw her again, and found her able to look after her family and support her husband's ministry with confidence, while her health was improving every day. She had found the answer to her needs in the healing power of Jesus.

!!!!!!!!!!!!!!!!!!!!!!!!!!!!!!!!!!!!!!!!!!!!!

# Wanstead, London

"I had never regarded myself as depressive, quite the opposite, until I was expecting our second child.

"My first pregnancy had been wonderful, but my second was dogged by bad health and mental stress from the outset.

"James was born at home three weeks before we moved into a house which needed more than a lick of paint to make it habitable. My husband, bless him, was working to get the worst jobs done, and as Jamie was two weeks late, my mother, who had offered to look after me, was on holiday.

"Nine days later Rachel had an accident; I was losing ground. I had imagined my depression would lift when we moved, but it was quite the reverse. I became easy prey to fits of uncontrollable temper; I would shout and scream and throw things.

"The child whom I loved dearly was my whipping-boy, and after that I would sit and sob in depression. I loathed what I'd become; every night I vowed tomorrow would see me patient and loving, yet every tomorrow was a nightmare of hysterical temper and self-condemnation. Then I tore a pillowcase in half during one of my bouts, and that night I begged the Lord to help me.

"A friend of mine had read of the St Paul's meeting, and, knowing I was seeking the Lord, asked me to go with her. I went expecting something, I don't know what, but certainly not to give my life to Christ. I returned home with a soggy handkerchief and splitting headache. That night I had virtually no sleep.

"Next morning my head was still pounding and I felt drained, but when I looked out into the garden I realised I was no longer alone — the Lord was with me; Jesus had taken away living death, and made me a gift of life and wonderful peace and joy in His love.

"That's it, the beginning I mean, for the Lord has blessed myself and my family, time and time again, in more ways than my appreciation can grasp. Praise Him that He does not barter His love as so many of us do, but gives it undeservedly and without reservation to all who seek Him."

✳ ✳ ✳ ✳ ✳ ✳ ✳ ✳ ✳ ✳ ✳ ✳

# Charles:

"I have received an incomparable blessing from the Lord through your ministry at High Leigh. For three years I have steadily deteriorated with depression to such an extent I was even envious of those in prison who were much better off than me, trapped in my own prison unable to communicate, receive love, or even think, and the Lord has given me a very fine brain.

"I was so unable to cope that I thought that all I could do was to go and lock myself away in an old people's retirement home with my few needs being done for me. For three years I have steadfastly continued reading my beloved Bible, even though it was so totally dead. It was really that dark night of the soul often written about by early Christians, and was pure hell.

"What made it worse was that I had to keep a bold front to all except my fellowship group and a few others. Now praise the Lord I am healed and have been leaping about like the lame man healed by Peter and John. My mind is clear, I can enjoy God's beauty again and feel His wonderful love. My Bible pours out living water into my heart."

# Miss C.M.S. Nottingham:

"I thought I'd write and tell you about a touch of healing I had at the service where you were ministering at on Wednesday evening at Bulwell Pentecostal Church. Mrs Dearing prayed for me as I've had nervous trouble for many years. I mentioned that I'd had a lot of stress due to the work I do with the charity I helped to start. Mrs Dearing prayed for me and during the prayer asked the Lord to heal me of the depression I'd had. I realised that the Lord must have guided you to ask this, Mrs Dearing, as I hadn't mentioned the depression I often used to get, especially when waking up in the morning. Since the prayer I've not had any depression at all.

"Some words that I believe the Lord gave me:

*Lord, I'm so grateful for all You're doing for me;*
*It'll take all of eternity to be able*
*to thank You enough for setting me free!*
*Free as the cotton-wool clouds in the sky;*
*As joyous as the burst and sparkle*
*of a thousand firework rockets,*
*their splendid colours racing*
*across the dark night*
*to shouts of glee and laughter from me!*

#### CHAPTER TWO

*Oh let me live <u>only</u> to be used by Thee,*
*To take the heavy dungeon-key,*
*And say to those in deep distress:*
*His way <u>is</u> best — just come and see!*
*He loves you so — come — and be free!"*

✳ ✳ ✳ ✳ ✳ ✳ ✳ ✳ ✳ ✳ ✳ ✳ ✳ ✳ ✳ ✳ ✳ ✳ ✳

# Mrs I.B., Preston:

"I was invited that evening to attend the Service at Hesketh Bank Methodist Chapel, where I hoped to discuss my problems with you, and that evening I did go forward, as I also had been a sufferer from depression for five years. I was set free!

"Now six weeks later I feel alive and have emerged from that dark tunnel of hell where I was for three years without even a glimmer of light."

# A.M., Sevenoaks:

"The Lord brought me to your meeting at City Hall. There Trevor was moved to ask my son and myself to come forward from our seats at the back of the gallery, as the Lord had a special ministry for us. You laid hands on us with prayer and I want you to know that I have been wonderfully released from deep fears which had been passed through several generations. I really feel NEW now and believe He has set me FREE. PRAISE HIM and thank you both."

# M.W.,Ware, Hertfordshire, 1998

"This is just a note to tell you how glad I was you came to Ware in April. I came to listen to Trevor's talk in the Full Gospel Church, and I went up afterwards for healing. Anne prayed for me — I asked for peace. I really experienced the presence of the Holy Spirit, and 'rested in the Spirit'. It was a very joyful experience and I felt a great peace.

"I have suffered from insomnia for many years, and usually took a sedative anti-depressant at night, which helped. Since Anne prayed for me I have slept most nights without taking any tablets, which is wonderful.

"May the Lord continue to bless you richly in your work for Him."

# Bridget, Mill Hill, London 1985

"Thank you so much for your kindness and help at the 'High Leigh' weekend. At last I found someone who <u>understood</u>.

"Now, whenever I feel a bit down about a problem, I turn to Trevor's book, 'God and Healing of the Mind', and start to look ahead and not back. In some ways I really do feel that I have escaped from the terrible prison of depression at last — and the fact that my friends can tell the difference helps!

"I had been having counselling sessions to help me over family problems, and to my surprise, have now been told that the need for this is ending!"

# Lesley, Chingford 1983

"I have never met you or even been to a meeting you held, but I have felt for a long time to get in touch with you. Thank you so much for your tapes; their ministry has been such a blessing to me. I know you will understand when I tell you how wonderful it feels to be free — I have been healed of agoraphobia. I couldn't understand why I wasn't healed immediately, but I do now, as I had many lessons to learn and a lot of growing to do. There were times when I felt very low and I would listen to a tape and would end up in front of the ironing board on my knees, in tears, just praising the Lord.

"Last summer I went away in fear and trembling, and the only thing that encouraged me to go was the fact that I was sure I was going to see one of your meetings advertised (I have heard your name mentioned time and time again). I didn't, of course, but obviously God knew what He was doing. I went to a Prayer, Praise and Healing meeting in October, and although I thought my phobias were my 'cross to bear', Someone pushed me forward. A small man named Jim [Rattenbury, who often ministered alongside us at St Paul's, Hainault] laid hands on me, and I felt no different. All that week I felt worse than I'd ever felt; then when I awoke on the Friday, I was healed.

"Thank you for being obedient and doing the Lord's work at Hainault. Many people are still being blessed, and although I wasn't there it's been a source of real encouragement to many people on their Christian walk."

# Bella, Tibshelf, Derby 1985

"I brought my daughter-in-law Molly and friend Peggy in 1980 to Holy Trinity Church, Matlock, for the laying-on of hands, for them to receive healing from our lovely Jesus. I had faith for both of them; they were such lost souls, full of pain and depressed.

"Both said in the car, 'Our faith is not great.' But I was so very sure. To me it was just like walking up to the front and you handing them a biscuit on a plate; they had only to reach out and take it and eat it. Jesus wants us all well and happy, not ill.

"Oh, the joy it gave my husband and myself that the Lord touched both of them that night! Molly was back delivering her babies a month later and is still working part-time on nights. She took her corset back to hospital and told them, 'Give it to somebody else; Jesus has healed my back.'

# M.W., Kettering 1996
## *(Addressed to Anne)*

This is just a few lines to say "thank you" to you for praying for me on Saturday — and "thank you" to you and your husband for coming over to Kettering and encouraging our friends there. My husband and I and our friend Richard (all from Oundle) were all blessed by the meeting — I should say by God, through the meeting. I believe I was delivered on Saturday night from something awful which has tormented me for many years.

I have attempted suicide seven times; the last time being in March this year. All these have been serious attempts, especially the last one. I took enough tablets to kill me, and wasn't found for a long time. Naturally speaking I should have died. But God spared my life.

God bless you both and strengthen you.

# Julie, Ilsington, Newton Abbot 1999

"I expect you thought I might never write. Well, I guess **I just wanted to be sure once I got home that the healing would continue** and I wouldn't go back to square one. Well, it was tough returning, but with Jesus' help and Christian fellowship I have been able to cope with the downs.

"I am attending counselling and although the past is painful to remember and relive, each session enables me with Jesus' help to put it in the past without feeling guilty or dirty.

"The last thing I expected on that first meeting was to be called forward by the Lord to start a week of healing and blessings. I am so grateful to you, Anne, for listening to the Lord and not giving up on me. You are very loving and caring and a great credit to the Lord.

"Although the first few days of that week were tough and spent mainly in tears, the Lord's words that you expressed, Trevor, really hit home, and your books played an important part in the healing process.

"I am sure I will never forget your love, concern and genuine kindness of that week. To have been brought from the depths of despair to such a glorious feeling can only be the work of the Lord and His faithful servants."

# Isabel, Tain 1990

"It was a great pleasure to be at Crieff and to meet you both at last. I had listened to so many of your tapes in the early days and of course read your books, 'Supernatural Superpowers' and 'Supernatural Healing Today'. I still have the former.

"I felt released from emotional hurts the afternoon you ministered, Anne. I sleep much better now and am coming off sleeping pills. It was all such a blessing but so short. Thank you both so much for coming!"

# Christine, Nr Swaffham 2003

(Christine's testimony is a little different — it tells of God's direct healing of emotional problems through her willingness to listen to Him with a repentant heart.):

"I was severely depressed, having had depression for some time and insomnia, and I had cried all morning, all afternoon and all evening until midnight — making me have red swollen eyes like a boxer's eyes! I had had depression for several years but it keeps coming back . . . Well, the Lord showed me at midnight that I had deep-seated resentment towards my Mum and through all the tears all day He was healing me of the inner deep hurts from revived memories of the mental and emotional torture that I had from my Mum.

"He spoke to me, saying that instead of thinking how horrible she is to me to keep hurting me (she is 92 and has hurt me since I was aged 7, and I am aged 63) the Lord said, 'Think how you have hurt her by all your great resentment to her.' I repented in tears again — just agony of repentance and felt so unworthy, thinking: how can He forgive me for this resentment? But He did forgive me, and such a release came. I stopped crying and felt such peace and joy of the Lord. I have not got the depression back and have been free of it for a few days now since the Lord did that miracle for me."

45

## Keith Dixon
## Secretary and Vice-President,
## Whitley Bay Chapter of the Full Gospel
## Business Men's Fellowship International

"I write on behalf of all the men of the Whitley Bay Chapter to thank you both most sincerely for the special time you spent with us. It can only be described as absolutely tremendous, in many kinds of ways.

". . . It has not been possible for me to consolidate all that happened, but one small thing which meant so much to my wife and myself was that my mother-in-law, bereaved earlier this year, who was formerly extremely reluctant to have anything to do with churches and thought we were all weird, has been touched by God. She has been explaining how peaceful she has been feeling and has talked extensively about the whole of the Friday evening she was at, and I know it is for her a new beginning. Having suffered from nerves and phobias for much of her life, it is remarkable she even came along to the dinner, but prayers worked, and the result is very pleasing."

# Margaret, Sandiacre

"You have spoken peace, rest and calm into my life. You have given me a glimpse of how to trust in God for living a completely restored and renewed life by the power of Jesus' shed blood and in the strength of His Spirit.

"I was ministered to by you, Anne, yesterday at St John's Church, Long Eaton. I experienced your gentle touch and heard the command for the pain in my head and neck to go. I believe that not only have I received the healing I was seeking, but more than that — a healing much deeper within my mind and emotions.

"May God receive the glory from your love and faithfulness in using the wonderful gifts He has entrusted to you both."

46

# Mary, infant school teacher

"Do you remember Mary, the infant school teacher I brought to you? You so kindly said, 'Come over straight away to my house' and you prayed for her in your kitchen. She was in a complete catatonic state and had been for weeks. As you prayed, God touched her and she awoke and opened up like a flower on those speeded-up film pictures. She was <u>cured</u>!"

C.T.

# Stephen, Bethnal Green 1998

"First of all my apologies for the delay in writing this letter since your talk nearly two years ago at the Women's Aglow guest meeting in the Bunting Rooms, Colchester, on September 21st, 1996.

"**But two years allows for a longer-term testimony of the healing I received so greatly** at that meeting - a once and for all experience.

"That summer I had been suffering from depression, following a breakdown at Easter. This was my fourth period of hospitalisation in a period of about eight years, since I first got mentally ill at the age of nineteen. The first time was the worst, and successive periods of treatment were mostly due to my taking myself off my medication — thinking I was doing alright on my own, and getting over-confident. However, this time I had got ill mostly due to the shock of seeing my Dad in hospital, so frail and ill, after a difficult operation to remove a brain tumour.

"I broke down trying to cope with this, and shortly afterwards went into hospital in Colchester, where my parents lived, and though I had lost touch with my local church there, some small part of me kept insisting: *'get help from church friends — not just psychiatrists!'*

"So I got back in touch with some old friends from church, who helped me get re-involved in a local housegroup. In this comfortable, Spirit-led, Scripture-based environment, my real healing began to slowly take place.

"At the height of summer, I thought I was recovered, so I set off back to London and University, to catch up on half a year's essays and exams before the next term started. Not surprisingly, I didn't manage it, and I realised my recovery needed more time, and I reluctantly agreed to spend more time in the hospital.

"Then, on September 9th, 1996, I got a call from the hospice where my Dad was staying, saying someone was coming to take me over to my family there, because my father had died. At that point, if I hadn't already, I could have hit rock bottom. Going on past records, I could have got a lot worse than *that*. However, God had things in hand, and I had reached a level of stability in my health by the time this happened.

"A week or so later, before it was really beginning to sink in, a good friend from church, a lady called Grace, asked me if I would like to go to the Women's Aglow meeting in town, as a guest on that day.

"That I got to the meeting at all was a miracle in itself. I took a bus on my own from the hospital, when I was feeling very fragile and insecure. When I got there, you seemed a very humble man, and you gave a talk about the healing in 'God's shop window'. But it wasn't so much the words you used as the sense of the Holy Spirit showing me something about *acceptance* — of my condition, my past periods of illness which I saw as failures, and also my Dad's illness and death.

"The talk ended and you were inviting people forward, and before my eyes there were people passing out, and dropping like ninepins! I thought, *I've heard of the Toronto blessing, but that's 'over there' . . .! What was all this?* Well, I was taken aback — it was the first time I'd actually seen such 'slayings' — but I *did* sense that it really was the Holy Spirit at work. God was here in this place, so anything going on in it must be allowed by God!

"Then the Holy Spirit pointed His finger at me, and told me I should go forward. Well, I guess I was a bit reluctant — I didn't fall down in the Spirit — but instead, you simply put your arm around me, which was the most loving gesture I can remember. You looked at me with gentle blue eyes, and said something like, 'I know what you've been going through. I've been there. But there is no going back — you won't go through it again — and I'll be praying for you.'

"I knew you had been there, but I wasn't so sure it wouldn't happen again — and if you found time to pray for me, I know God will return the favour! But your words of encouragement sank into my spirit, and I began to believe that I will not get ill again; slowly at first, then more so, like the little mustard seed.

"Not long after, God opened my mind to just how much He had been with me throughout that period since Easter. He gave me a kind of revelation as to just how closely He had been directing my paths — through lonely nights of anxiety in the hospital; to the doors of Christian friends again at church; to make friends with one or two faces in the ward as well as getting so much support from the staff nurses, sympathetic doctors and counsellors; how I'd ended up in Colchester near my family and my father; and how his operation and health had given him the whole summer at home, in a stable condition, with all his family around.

"Most of all, these things had come together so that I could make up with my Dad, who had not spoken to me since a falling out two years earlier. Because of the extra lease of life God gave him, I was able to make up with him and forgive him — that summer we chatted more than ever before, and had some really special, and funny moments together.

"When he died peacefully that September, the Lord really gave me a sense of peace through having made up with my Dad — I don't think I could ever have accepted the loss if it had happened any other way. God's intervention brought us reconciliation and a sense of true peace and comfort in my heart.

"I was discharged the next month, got a Christmas job locally, then returned to studies in London in the New Year of '97. This June I take my Finals to complete my degree in Psychology — but I don't think I'm much the wiser . . . ! And, more than this, I got married to Susan on St Valentine's Day of this year, our engagement having survived my getting ill. Susan is a wonderful woman, and it always amazes me how God matched us together at every level.

"And I can confirm that this two years has been the longest period of 'remission', as the doctors would say, since my illness. *Remission?* Rubbish! I say, *'New Creation!!!'* I'm walking in wholeness, and it's here to stay!!

"Trevor, I just want to say an overdue, heartfelt thanks for your being such an influential part in the start of my journey into wholeness. It is with thanks and rejoicing that I can say the words of Psalm 40 have become my testimony:

*I waited patiently for the Lord;*
*He turned to me and heard my cry.*
*He lifted me out of the slimy pit,*
*Out of the mud and mire.*
*He set my feet on a rock*
*And gave me a firm place to stand.*
*He put a new song in my mouth,*
*a hymn of praise to our God.*
*Many will see and fear,*
*And put their trust in the Lord.*

Psalm 40: 1-3.

"I just want to bless you by letting you know that God has used you in a very powerful and touching way in my life."

# Finally, a letter from America

Rabab — written from Greece,
but about our ministry in Seattle:

"Greetings from Greece! I am from St Luke's, Seattle, WN. We were not too closely associated, though one in the Spirit! Presently I am on vacation in Greece.

"Ever since you moved back to England I have wanted to write. I have waited so long, and now it is nice to have plenty of time to write to family and friends and dear people like you. I thank God for pen and paper, for without it we would not even have His written word. But I don't know if I can sufficiently express in words to you my gratitude and praise to God for your time and ministry in Seattle, and please bear with my American English!

"Over the years since you left I have believed the Holy Spirit has shown you both how beautifully your lives touched so many. I had just returned from Greece in 1980, and shortly afterwards the Lord sent you to us. I don't think I can exaggerate how precious your time with us was. You have both ministered to so many lost and broken souls — now saints ministering to one another.

"Well, I was certainly one more. On the surface my life looked very well; I am a good actress! Inside I was quite desperate, with no end in sight. During many of the Sunday services I was with the preschool age children, but God's love flowed through your ministry and broke through areas of my being, to begin healing my brokenness.

"God has never held back any good thing from me. He has given me so many blessings in so many ways. My stumblingblock has been myself, and allowing God to redeem my soul. I have put up so many walls. I have needed to learn to love myself also. I have felt so unworthy and my self-condemnation and hatred have grieved God's heart. As I am writing this I am reminded of the new heart He has given us. Old things are passed away, all things shall become new.

"And a still small voice reminds me of those precious words of knowledge and love given to His church through your ministry. Which I also received — at times I felt it was only for myself and God speaking directly to me. His love began to melt my frightened, broken heart.

"I have known more of God's mercy and grace and the intimacy and fellowship of His holiness because of your ministry. I still have a long way to go; I suppose I am working out my salvation. I know He is faithful — remember the song you loved: 'Great is Thy faithfulness, morning by morning new mercies I see . . . ' He is ever ready to carry our burdens, keep and lead us through it all!

"When I think of the love that shone through your lives, and how much greater God's love must be, it makes me cry for joy. I never want to forget the day I received Jesus like a child with many tears of repentance and praise. To know His mercy and grace. I want so to believe completely that I will spend eternity with Him.

"There were a lot of people left wondering why God took you away from St Luke's. He is the Lord; He is sovereign. I truly believe God knew from before time began that He would send you both to His flock in Ballard for a season! The fruit of your labor was tremendous joy and love, and I could go on and on! The people fell so in love with you that it was painful at first to understand God's plan to lead us all on. But He knew from the beginning; many, including myself, had our eyes on your ministry. During the weeks and months after you left I had visions of you before the Great Shepherd, resting in His eternal love. Many lost sheep came to know the Shepherd of their souls through your example. Including me."

*        *        *        *        *        *        *

We have met Christians who assert that believers should never be emotionally ill, but enjoy God's peace and joy all the time, or at least, most of it. They can understand that unbelievers may suffer depression and fear, but believe that when a person is in Christ; a new creation, emotional problems and illnesses should be left behind. Because of this teaching, in our experience many emotionally ill Christians have felt guilty because of their illness.

However, even if we are Christians, we are still human beings, living in an imperfect world, and the people in it, as well as chemical imbalances, or hormonal problems, can still cause Christians to be emotionally ill. Our experience is that God accepts this and does not reject His emotionally ill children, whether believers or not. Doctors, psychiatrists and psychotherapists find these emotional conditions difficult to heal. Medicine can help, but rarely heals. God, however, definitely has compassion on the emotionally sick and reaches out to pour His loving, healing balm into the deep recesses of their being — result — miracles.

---

# *Part Two*

---

## Miracles through
## the use of the voice

# 3

# God's use of the spoken word

Human words have power, whether written or spoken. They can encourage, bless and help, or hurt, wound or even destroy the ones to whom they are addressed. They can be like bullets fired from a gun to penetrate and explode within their target. Words written in the Bible, God's word, have changed the lives of many readers for the better.

Preachers' words, anointed by the Holy Spirit, have brought about conversion, new birth and an entry into a relationship with God for over two thousand years. Christians are familiar with and believe in the power of the words of the Bible or words spoken in the name of God.

Not all, however, have appreciated God's use of the power of the spoken word to bring miracles of healing to the body and mind of sick people. Yet Jesus often spoke healing to those who sought His help, using such words as: "Receive your sight" to the blind, or "Be clean!" to lepers, or "Your sins are forgiven" to the guilty.

We have followed this example and teaching in our ministry, frequently with amazing miracles resulting from our prayerful and power-ful commands for the sick to be healed. Here are a few examples of God's use of the spoken word to convey healing to the afflicted.

# Nanette

It was the "word" which was so effective in the case of Nanette Pierce. This lady, a dark, pretty young woman, was married, with two children. She was wheeled into a meeting suffering from terminal cancer. Her tragic condition was well known in her home town of Peterborough because the local newspaper had issued a special appeal to readers to bring her home from the USA so that she could die and be buried here.

However, some months later the same newspaper carried a front-page headline:

# MIRACLE

Reporters described how this lady was no longer expected to die. After she attended one of our meetings, doctors discovered that all traces of the disease had disappeared.

She told newspaper reporters that the change had actually taken place when Trevor had gone over to her and commanded, "Rise and walk, in the name of Jesus!"

"I couldn't help but obey him," she confessed. "I just got up!" So, a lady who looked such a pathetic wreck, rendered paralysed by cancer, stood and then walked, for the glory of God. She had heard the word of God, unhesitatingly responded, and been healed. As an added bonus, her hair, which she had completely lost, immediately began to grow again. Her progress continued.

Other cancers have also shrivelled up under the power of this ministry. In the name of Jesus, and with His word upon his lips, Trevor has often addressed organs of the body and commanded them to respond to the healing power of Jesus. Healing has often resulted.

"Prostate gland, be healed!" he once cried. The patient, who had been passing blood, later wrote:

> I went into hospital for an exploration of my bladder. This was two months ago. Today I had to go to the hospital and was told I had a clean bill of health. Praise the Lord.

Similarly, Trevor has sometimes rebuked sicknesses in the name of Jesus and commanded them to depart. Arthritis, in particular, has yielded to this treatment. One lady wrote:

I was taken ill with severe arthritis of the spine in June of last year and, in spite of various hospital treatments, my position got worse, culminating in the Royal Free Hospital in London sending me here unable to help me in any way. I came to your mission at Wisbech. I am now greatly relieved. My family think a miracle has happened and I am greatly blessed.

✤ ✤ ✤ ✤ ✤ ✤ ✤ ✤ ✤ ✤ ✤ ✤ ✤ ✤ ✤ ✤ ✤ ✤ ✤ ✤ ✤

58

# "I can speak!" Plymouth

Anne doesn't remember exactly whether she laid hands on the man who stood in front of her and pointed to his throat. She says:

"I realised that there was something wrong with his throat, and I just looked into his eyes, and said, 'Lord, heal this man now.' I don't remember whether I put my hands on his head, but I remember how surprised we both were, when he said, 'I can speak!'

"It happened so quickly. I was amazed, and shared his excitement that he could use his voice. He was saying, 'Thank you, thank you! I'm all right! I can talk! Thank you! Thank you!'

"After the service the man came up to me and just said, 'Thank you! It's wonderful!' "

# Olive, Saffron Walden

"I am just writing to say how much the Lord blessed me through your ministry at the Women's Aglow meeting last Saturday. When you placed your hand on me and pronounced that I was a completely free woman I felt the power of the Lord through my whole body, and I found myself telling Jesus how much I loved Him.

"Thank you very much for the joy that the Lord has given me through your ministry."

\*   \*   \*   \*   \*   \*   \*

On one occasion Trevor's words to a woman were: "You need to step out into the glorious liberty God has given you through His love."

*In due course a letter arrived from her daughter:*

59

"My mother, who was suffering from depression, was taking many drugs, tranquillisers, sleeping pills, etc. She stopped them due to your words and has been completely healed."

The spoken word has also been of great benefit to those who have responded to the appeal Trevor always makes after the gospel message at our meetings. After they have expressed penitence for their sins and received Jesus as their Saviour, Trevor has been able to say: "On the authority of the Word of God. I am able to declare confidently to each one of you that your sins have been forgiven. You stand there in garments as white as snow, for 'If we confess our sins, he is faithful and just and will forgive us our sins and purify us from all unrighteousness' " (1 John 1: 9).

This was so in the case of a girl named Jacky, who was the first person to come forward in response to the appeal at a rally in Southend, Essex. She was known throughout the school for her uncontrollable temper, which resulted in her being expelled by the headmaster.

After Trevor's words to her the change in her was truly wonderful. Even unbelievers exclaimed, "Well! You *have* changed, Jacky!" She was so thrilled that people were noticing the difference. Eventually the school took this transformed young person back again.

Another convert found healing as a direct result of receiving the forgiveness and new life of Christ. She wrote:

My body was becoming distorted with drugs, overeating and lack of exercise. I wasn't a nice person either. Then you told me about Jesus and I accepted Him as my Saviour. Things started to change! I started to change from the inside. The injections have been stopped – the anti-depressants and sedatives went down the drain.

# Wallingford

"I felt God say to write to you and thank you for your words to us about our daughter. In 1980 when aged 14 months she was in a harness after contracting septic arthritis of the right hip, with the possibility of never walking again. *The ball joint had been destroyed*, but you gave us faith to believe that she would walk again with no limp or sign of disability.

"At a meeting in Wallingford Church which I have recently been given a tape of, you said to my husband:

'Just believe and you'll see it.'

"Yesterday we had a telephone call from our daughter to say that she was vice-captain of the netball team at her university. She is a gymnast as well, able to do the splits and has won medals for her displays at Sports Acrobatic competitions."

Sometimes, when Trevor felt led to do so, he would ask people at meetings to stand if they were suffering from a certain sickness or perhaps some adverse circumstances, and he would encourage them to receive their healing from the Lord. Such was the case with Mrs C.F. at Tunbridge Wells:

"You told us to stand up if we suffered with migraines. You told me to move into the aisle. I vaguely remember doing this and holding on to the end of the pew, then I let go and you told someone to stand behind me and to touch me on the shoulder lightly, which I felt, then you started praying and my knees went. The next thing I remember was lying on the ground and several people round me. When I started to get up a lady got hold of my right arm and I said: 'No, that one is injured'.

"It had happened nine months previously. The radius bone went 2 inches out of the elbow with a compound fracture of the head of the radius; I tore all the tendons, muscles and some veins. I had the head of the radius bone removed about 6 weeks later and was told by the surgeon that I will never have 100% use back again. — I remember looking him in the eye and saying, 'OK if you say I have to accept that as fact, 99¾% will do and nothing less.' Last time I saw him, three months ago, he said that for the time since he operated it had healed way beyond his wildest dreams (hands had been laid on several times).

"I know that the Lord has cured me of the 24- and 48-hour migraines — now we have to wait at least six months to prove it medically. Thank you for being a channel for God's healing."

\*    \*    \*    \*    \*    \*    \*

So we see that, in the Christian ministry of healing, what we say, not only to God, but also to the sick and spiritually needy are *very* important and have the effect of producing miracles in those who receive them in faith.

# 4

## God's use of the "word of knowledge"

We were sitting on the front pews of an Anglican Church in Boston, England, in 1993, joining in the praise and worship which were to precede Trevor's preaching and our joint ministry to the sick, when a most remarkable testimony to God's healing power was given.

The man and his wife who were leading the worship by playing their guitars and singing also sang beautiful duets to inspire the congregation. It was in the middle of one such song that the man stopped and said:

"We would not be doing this if it were not for Trevor Dearing." He continued by relating how he and his wife had several years before undergone a terrible tragedy. Their little boy had been drowned in a swimming pool. This had caused them to be very resentful and bitter towards God and they would have nothing to do with Christianity.

However, it had apparently been advertised that Trevor would be conducting a healing meeting in a neighbouring town to where they lived, and a neighbour had persuaded them to go to hear this "well known" speaker. No sooner had they entered that particular church when Trevor, who, in the natural, did not know them or their tragedy, said:

"God has just told me that there is a man and his wife here who are in deep grief and resentment towards God because their little boy was drowned in a swimming pool. The Holy Spirit has told me to tell them that their son is wonderfully happy with Jesus and doesn't want them to be in sorrow and grief."

The couple were overwhelmed with amazement and joy at the utterance of words about a situation of which Trevor had no previous knowledge, and they opened their hearts to receive God's love in Jesus Christ.

It was soon discovered by their pastor, after they had joined a church, that they had a wonderful musical gift, and so their nationwide singing ministry had begun.

Both Anne and Trevor have often had such supernatural knowledge given to them by the Holy Spirit, and when we have spoken out such words, in faith, God has used them for miracles of healing. Such has been the case in the following:

# The London teacher

Pat, who was an infant school teacher in London, was brought to Trevor suffering from intense depression. It had started after the death of her father, with whom she lived.

Trevor remembers: "When she came to the vicarage, her neurosis was so severe that she was unable to communicate. She sat on the office sofa sagging like a rag doll with her head between her knees. She had been in this condition for several days, and her doctor had agreed that Christian friends should bring her to Hainault.

"My attempts to counsel her were useless, as she would not answer my questions. I began to pray for her, and as I did so, the Lord showed me clearly the details of her problems. I began

64

to tell her all that Jesus was making known to me, that He knew her needs and was answering them.

"Promise after promise came to her from the Lord through my lips. In the end I commanded her to come out of her 'prison house', and break the chains in which Satan had imprisoned her.

"She later told us that the very next morning, instead of being taken to a mental hospital, she was back at school, teaching her class of energetic children."

!!!!!!!!!!!!!!!!!!!!!!!!!!!!!!!!!!!!!!!!!!!

Trevor explains: "When I am privileged to be used in this ministry, I stand, with my eyes closed, deeply concentrated and wonderfully aware of God. I have no control over how long this will continue before I am brought back to earth. I usually then ask people who know that they have been healed to stand and thank the Lord.

"Sometimes, however, it happens that healed people just cannot restrain themselves from immediately praising the Lord.

" 'My foot! My foot! I can move it! I really can!' shouted an excited girl in a marquee at Cheadle where I was ministering.

"Her club foot had not moved since the day she was born, and she was awaiting an operation which had only a slight chance of success.

"At one meeting, at Wolverhampton, I received ten such words of knowledge, and all of them were verified before I left the area the following day.

"Generally however, I like time to pass, to make sure that the miracles are genuine, for Jesus' sake. This usually means that people write to me after a mission is over. Here is a sample letter:"

# Wisbech healing

This lady wrote:

"I would like to pass on some news of a miracle of healing that came to me at Wisbech, when, by word of knowledge, you described my symptoms.

"After keeping away from doctors for three years, I suddenly needed six within the space of three months, and was taken ill twice when away from home and had to send for help. Constant bilious attacks, a colitis condition, and agonising pain in the small of the back — sometimes causing me to lie on the floor to try to find a position to be out of pain.

"The night before Wisbech I spent hours with a 'waterworks' condition, exactly as you described it. From the moment you mentioned these symptoms they vanished completely. I still did not believe it and had already arranged for a checkup in the R.A.F. hospital. After a week of intensive investigations they pronounced me completely free and healthy.

"All praise once more to our fantastic Heavenly Physician."

# Canvey Island

Mrs S.N. of Basildon wrote to say that she had healing of memories through a word of knowledge on Canvey Island. She had been distressed for years by the memory of the loss of her son. Now she has peace.

# Stoke on Trent

A letter from Stoke on Trent described how Trevor had revealed, through a word of knowledge, the healing of four major illnesses. It continued:

"You also discovered a bad chain forged between a mother and child — which you promised would be broken and you said 'there will be nothing but love from now on.' That chain had been growing thicker and heavier for years between my daughter and me. She came home for Christmas and the love has been wonderful."

And another:
"We praise the Lord for the wonderful disappearance of a lump in a lady's breast which was feared to be malignant. By word of knowledge you said it would go — and it has!"

# Halesowen, West Midlands

Paul writes:

"My wife was especially blessed by your special word for her on Saturday evening. She had already been forward for healing regarding her bladder problem (i.e. getting up three to four times in the night). Since your ministry, no problems. Praise the Lord."

# From Spalding:

"You said, 'There is a person here suffering from sinus trouble for fifteen years.' That was me. You declared me healed so I threw away my nose drops. The sickness just went. Praise the Lord."

# M.E. healed, Harrogate

"I just want to say how much I enjoyed your visit to St Andrew's Church. Also to say how God mightily used you in healing my friend's daughter of M.E. It was at the end of the meeting on the Sunday evening that you had a word of knowledge and announced that Catherine with M.E. was healed. She had been in a wheelchair, and no longer is now. Hallelujah!"

Mrs D.R.

# Stamford:
## The healing of Dennis Rose

"In November 1973 at the age of 44 years I became seriously ill with kidney problems and was taken to Stamford hospital, where I remained for 12 days. In the weeks that followed I was in great pain and feeling very weak. I began to despair of ever feeling well again. Having always been strong and healthy this was a new dimension in my life.

"One Friday I was reading the Stamford and Rutland Mercury, and in it was the following:

# Divine Healing Service in the
Congregational Hall, Stamford,
led by the Reverend Trevor Dearing

"I was not very keen on going, but I felt so ill I was prepared to try anything. My doctor was doing his best to help me, but to no avail. I told my wife Iris about the advertisement I had seen in the paper and she was not at all interested. She wanted me to be perfectly well again but did not want to be involved in that sort of ministry. All through her life she had been staunch Church of England, and liked the comfort and dignity that went with the Service.

68

"On the 7 mile journey I kept wondering if I was doing the right thing, for I was also Church of England though not as staunch as my wife. I arrived at the meeting at 7.00 pm for the 7.30 start. The Congregational Hall was filled very quickly. I sat at the back, ready to make my escape. I still hadn't convinced myself I had done the right thing. I really was very nervous.

"What followed was wonderful. Trevor Dearing began the service with prayers that made me realise that here was something special. They were spiritually uplifting. The tone was set, the chorus and hymn singing divine, and for almost two hours Trevor preached about the love of Jesus for mankind. It was a joy to listen to him, and as the words flowed he made the New Testament come alive.

"This was followed by the laying on of hands. People just fell down under the power of the ministry given by Anne and Trevor Dearing. This was the Lord's work through the power of the Holy Spirit. I witnessed many wonderful things and it was too much for me to understand. I did not go forward for ministry, still being too nervous. This was all new to me and I returned home amazed at what I had seen.

"I repeatedly spoke about what I had witnessed and was longing for the next service in a month's time. I went to the following three services and was still afraid to go forward for the laying on of hands, although I was still in a lot of pain and feeling ill, not knowing how I would feel after the ministry.

"My wife finally agreed very reluctantly to come with me in case it was necessary for her to drive me home. This was the fourth meeting and I was going forward for the laying on of hands. Iris and I arrived at the Congregational Hall and it was full. Many people were ill and in great need, and I was one of them. The meeting started. After prayers, choruses and hymns Trevor started to speak about the needs of the sick and suffering people. He suddenly stopped and said, 'There is someone in the congregation who is in great pain on the left side below the rib cage and has been ill for a considerable time.' He also said that the person had been afraid to come forward, but that the Lord was healing him right where he was, and there was no need to come forward.

"I knew immediately that that person was me. I felt a warmth go through my body from my head to my feet and all my pain went with it. Within a very short space of time my feelings of illness went also. I must also mention that prior to Trevor's word I had noticed that Iris was raising her hands in praise to the Lord. She said that she had never seen or heard anything so spiritually uplifting as the singing and outpouring of praise as she witnessed in the Congregational Hall on this her first visit. We praised the Lord at that evening service and continue to praise Him to this day.

"I informed Trevor of my healing and that his word of knowledge had been for me. Iris and I continued to attend the monthly services, becoming more d more involved with the passage of time. I was privileged to be used in stewardship and ministry at many meetings. We continue to serve the Lord and so witness His Divine healing and blessing on many people's lives. The meetings were a period in our lives which brought us great joy and a deeper awareness of the presence of the Lord. The glory is the Lord's. To the Father, Son and Holy Spirit be all honour, glory and power, praise and dominion for ever!"

This ministry has been described as "healing by remote control", so the following probably fits best in this section:

# Pauline: – "a bit scary"

"I am presently reading 'Called to Be a Wife'. I didn't at first find the book inspiring but suddenly as I was reading it I began to weep. God is indeed so good! So thank you for taking the time and getting up the courage to put your life in print.

"Also dear Trevor, we have actually met – you spoke at a meeting in Wycliffe church a few years ago, and through God's power He used your ministry to heal me completely, which was rather fine as I was crippled with a pelvis injury at the time. I hadn't even gone up for prayer as I found you a bit scary, but God touched me anyway. Praise Him."

❋ ❋ ❋ ❋ ❋ ❋ ❋ ❋ ❋ ❋ ❋ ❋ ❋ ❋ ❋ ❋ ❋ ❋ ❋

Sometimes the "word of knowledge" is given through another gift — that of speaking in tongues through the Holy Spirit. The following is an example of a miracle brought about in this way:

# Speaking in tongues, Switzerland

Anne remembers:

Another remarkable incident took place when I was ministering with Trevor at a World Conference of the Holy Spirit in Switzerland. Many hundreds of people had gathered to hear Trevor preach and then move into healing ministry. I took my place by his side and began to minister likewise. Many nations and languages were represented, so we couldn't always make use of an interpreter.

The next day two ladies approached me after breakfast. One spoke both Spanish and English fluently; the other spoke no English at all. I was asked if I spoke Spanish and, of course, replied in the negative.

"That's remarkable!" exclaimed the English-speaking lady, "truly a miracle has happened!"

"You see," she explained, "my Spanish friend here came to you for ministry and without asking her any questions, you began to pray for her bad back. You also told her that she was suffering from depression because of a curse on her life due to the fact that her mother had been a spiritist medium. You set her free from that curse and today she is a different person. She only came to the Conference as an observer, but has now accepted Jesus Christ as her personal Saviour. She has been convinced of God's power because she understood every word you said; she heard you in Spanish!"

In the "natural" I cannot speak a word of Spanish at all! It had been just like the miracle of tongues at Pentecost all over again. The Spanish lady had also been wonderfully healed by the power of God.

# J.C., Midhurst

"I know you have been in touch with Stephen Cox, my closest friend in Jesus, whose back was healed after some 35 years through the power of the Holy Spirit through you. He had been in such awful debilitating pain for so long that I almost cried with joy when he was delivered from this deep affliction.

"On the same evening at the Full Gospel Business Men's meeting in Midhurst but somewhat earlier, as you started your healing ministry, you had a word for someone with heart problems. That was me — I had had angina for many years and it was a continuous nagging and unpleasant pain. When you prayed for me I went over like a ninepin in the Spirit, the first time for many years, and that in itself was wonderful. Almost immediately I noticed that my angina had been healed, but I thought it was more prudent to keep my counsel and ensure that it was a long term healing. But over the next few days, then weeks, then months the healing stuck even when I did something like drink white wine or rarely champagne.

"It is now six months at least since this happened and the Lord who is faithful has kept me healed, praised be His Name. I thought you would like to know this and thank you deeply for your part in it — for being faithful and obedient. May the Lord bless you in your turn."

\*　\*　\*　\*　\*　\*　\*

This "word of knowledge" was used by Jesus, in his discourse with the Samaritan woman at Jacob's well (John 4) and by Peter in the early Church (Acts 5). It is a gift promised to Spirit-filled believers mentioned by Paul in his first letter to the Corinthians (Chapter 12). It is a miracle in itself and is sent by God to effect miracles of healing.

# 5

## *God's use of the authoritative word*

When Trevor and Anne arrived at Hainault in September, 1970, with its very small congregation, mainly of very ordinary East London people, who had moved into this overspill estate, they could never have foreseen the extraordinary events that were to take place, in which exorcism played a part.

Trevor remembers one particular evening:

A wave of expectancy swept over me when, almost as if on cue, Denise, a 21-year-old prostitute stood up and screamed: "Jesus is dead. I saw him die."

I was about to start the weekly Tuesday evening power, praise and healing service, when dark-haired Denise stood up in front of what had now each Tuesday grown to a 500-plus congregation.

"No, no, I won't go out of her!" an unearthly voice inside her shouted.

The 10-minute drama was witnessed not only by the congregation, but by television cameras and an army of press people.

The news media were out in force following the trial of 31-year-old Michael Taylor, who savaged his wife to death after an all-night exorcism in the vestry of a village church in solid Yorkshire.

News had quickly spread to Fleet Street about what was happening at my red-brick Anglican church in the heart of a huge post-war housing estate just outside London.

Exorcism had suddenly become the topic on the lips of the British nation. Bishops banned it, drinkers argued about it over frothy pints in the pubs, and the Church was split over it, with some clergy saying it was a step back to the Dark Ages and others saying it was part of Christ's ministry while on earth, and why shouldn't it continue today?

I knew Denise from the previous Tuesday when she had screamed blue murder during the service. She had defeated all psychiatric efforts, but I believed I could help.

Determinedly I laid hands on her, and an other-world voice came from within her screaming, "No, no, don't cast me out!" I took authority over the spirit and a deadly conflict followed.

"Jesus is alive!" I cried. "Go, mocking spirit!"

The girl, who had been involved in spiritist activities, slumped to the floor. She had also been offering herself for prostitution in order to buy alcohol.

I took Denise, who was screaming, in my hands and asked the congregation: "Can we all pray for Denise? I am going to minister to her. Will you all sing quietly, 'Jesus Breaks Every Fetter'."

The atmosphere was electric as the congregation began singing and I again laid my hands on the shaking girl's head and said firmly: "I come now to cast you out."

After a couple of minutes during which the singing and praying grew louder, I encouraged those who were supporting me in this way by disclosing, with absolute confidence, "This spirit is going to the pit." I added: "I command you, in the name of Jesus! I forbid you to speak this blasphemy! You shall go out of the body of this woman. You shall not hurt this girl or anyone else any more. Go, in the name of Jesus!"

Then I shouted: "Out!"

Denise became relaxed, silent, and at peace. She looked flushed, dazed and weak, and was taken quickly from the church to escape an avalanche of journalists.

Later, Lancashire-born Denise told a Daily Mirror reporter that she felt the exorcism had changed her life, which she now wanted to dedicate to Christ.

Denise had, in fact, begun to scream 15 minutes before the service was due to begin, and it had been immediately obvious that I had either to minister deliverance to her or she would have to be dragged unceremoniously from the church. I chose the former alternative. The press had assembled with me at the front of the church for pre-service photographs and interviews and were beautifully positioned for the exorcism.

The next day the newspapers devoted a lot of space to the incident, and ever since I have been dubbed the "Exorcist Vicar", a title which gives a totally unbalanced picture of the scope of my ministry.

The Daily Mail reported: "About 500 people rolled up last night to watch a vicar 'give the devil the boot'.

"And they weren't disappointed. Dead on cue, in front of television cameras, reporters and scrambling photographers, a scream shattered the joyful singing.

"Then, as though a film director had shouted 'Cameras roll,' the trendy, long-haired Rev. Trevor Dearing in purple pullover and tartan trews, stepped into the limelight at St Paul's Church, Hainault, Essex.

76

"For Mr Dearing's speciality is exorcism — which because he doesn't want to get his marching orders from the Bishop, he prefers to call — 'deliverance'.

"Half-an-hour earlier in his attractively furnished vicarage next to the red brick church, the 42-year-old ex-accountant, who claims to have exorcised a thousand demons in the past four years, was preparing for a 'routine night'.

"It was hardly that. Within a few minutes of his walking in front of the hymn-singing congregation, a former alcoholic prostitute named Denise, aged 21, began screaming."

The reporter then described the exorcism in vivid detail.

The Daily Telegraph added: "The Bishop of Chelmsford, the Rt. Rev. Trillo, said yesterday that he intended 'at the earliest opportunity' to attend the regular weekly services at St. Paul's Church, Hainault, Essex, at which people are publicly exorcised.

"At a service in the church on Tuesday, attended by over 500 people and in front of television cameras, a 21-year-old former prostitute named Denise was 'delivered from demons' by the vicar, the Rev. Dearing, as she writhed and screamed in the aisle.

"Mr. Dearing, 42, who has carried out the healing and deliverance sessions at the tiny church in Arrowsmith Road since he was inducted there in 1970, claimed that Denise was possessed by evil spirits of mockery and lying."

The network Thames Television "This Week" documentary about our work at St Paul's, which included an interview with the Bishop of Chelmsford declaring his support for my ministry, was shown on Independent Television throughout the British Isles ten days later. For a long time afterwards I became the focal point of misunderstanding, debate, misrepresentation and pilgrim-ages from around Britain concerning exorcism.

It is difficult to exaggerate the repercussions of all this media coverage on St Paul's Church and on myself. However I was thankful to God that the press had seen a ministry of deliverance in the classic New Testament mould — and had seen that it worked.

Denise was interviewed by a reporter next day. She was relaxed and happy, holding a Bible and speaking about a new life that had now opened up for her.

She told Frank Thorne of the Daily Express that her troubles began after she dabbled with ouija boards.

He wrote that the "chubby 21-year-old" believed she became possessed by demons after trying to get spirit messages from an ouija board, an occult game which has a board covered with letters and numbers. The players put their fingers on a wineglass or a movable pointer and it "spells out" words in response to questions, supposedly from the dead.

"At school we used to play ouija all the time for a giggle," she told Thorne.

"We thought it was a joke until the day all the windows in the house blew open. Then we were scared stiff."

Denise said relations with her parents became strained. At the age of 17 she ran away from home in Preston, Lancs., and went to London

Frank Thorne's article continued: "She often slept rough. She had no job, but found there was easy money in prostitution. At night she hung around bars, drinking heavily.

" 'The more I drank, the more money I needed to earn on the game [prostitution]. It was a horrible life,' she said.

"Twice Denise tried to commit suicide by taking overdoses of tablets. All psychiatric attempts at help failed. Denise had first come to Trevor Dearing seven months previously. He had prayed for her but she drifted back to the bad life.

"After the exorcism she said: 'Thank God it's all over. I'm cleared of the devil.'

"Denise affirmed: 'I don't remember much because I went unconscious when Mr Dearing put his hands on me. I remember screaming. I was crying and I felt queer. It was no fake.' "

Just to make sure the very last demon had been cast out, I conducted a final exorcism – a small private ceremony of quiet prayer. There was no screaming this time. It simply confirmed what had happened that Tuesday night, when the ministry had been spontaneous, brief and effective.

The publicity brought many needy people to St Paul's who were either genuinely possessed or were just crying out for attention, and imitated possession by evil spirits. But however they came, they heard the gospel of Jesus Christ, and many turned to the Lord to answer their needs.

Deliverance ministry became a common part of the miracles God wrought through Trevor – and delivering a person from the devil's power and control certainly is a major miracle!

Demonic powers, once they have a grip on someone or have actually entered their inmost being, cause havoc in the sufferer's life. In the New Testament, and our experiences have authenticated (if such were needed by a modern-day doubter), demons can cause such things as spiritual and emotional torment, nightmares, horrific visions, hearing voices, depression, panic, fear, and even the physical symptoms of blindness, deafness, dumbness, spinal problems, and all manner of other physical effects. Once the demon or demons have been driven out of a person's life, however, he or she is *immediately* freed from their problem. It is miraculous.

Such deliverance of an oppressed, tormented or "possessed" person rarely involves the laying-on of hands. Even if such ministry is used, the deliverance is actually effected by an **authoritative word** of command for the demons to get out (be cast out) of the sufferer's life, in the **name of Jesus of Nazareth**, from whom the minister's authority is derived, and

79

whose authority they must obey through their defeat by Jesus' Person, crucifixion, resurrection and ascension.

However, the demons do sometimes offer resistance to the authoritative word, and always are unwilling to depart. The resulting manifestations can be hair-raising for a congregation who happen to be present; but nothing demonstrates the power and authority of the risen Christ more explicitly than effective deliverance ministry. This is shown by the following accounts.

By 1976 I (Trevor) had cast out of possessed people more than 1,000 demons in the previous few years, and in almost every case the tormented souls had a direct connection with the occult. These people had played with the devil and he had trapped them in his snares.

So when I was given the chance to invade what I regarded as occult territory – Ilford Spiritualist Church had invited me to lecture there on Divine healing – I was glad to take up the challenge. I had long opposed spiritism, (Leviticus 19: 31) but I felt this was a wonderful opportunity to witness to the vastly superior power of the Lord Jesus Christ over all occult bondage.

I told the mainly middle-aged audience that I believed it was Jesus alone who could heal the sick and set them free, and that He was my only guide in the supernatural realm. I said that I was His minister and not in any way a medium. It was a very challenging occasion.

One medium asked, "Have you a guide to the other side?"

"Yes. Most certainly," I replied.

"Is he powerful?" she asked, looking excited.

"Supremely so," I declared.

"Do you know his name?"

"Yes. Jesus Christ! I know Him very well. All my healing ministry is in his name. He heals. I'm his servant."

She showed surprise when I then said, "I wish you knew Jesus, too, then you would realise that there is no need of anyone else to guide you."

Several members afterwards expressed a desire to know Jesus personally, and three of them, including "Mary", a widow, turned up at one of my services at Hainault.

"I'm having horrific visions and hideous manifestations since I've tried to become a medium," she told me. "I'm desperate to be set free. Please help me, vicar."

So I prayed with her and one of the others who had come with her, and they accepted Christ as their Saviour, and then received the Baptism of the Holy Spirit. Mary was delivered from her hellish experience, and shortly afterwards I introduced her to another believer. Later I had the privilege of conducting their wedding ceremony.

They were the first of many former spiritualists who were converted to Christ, and received the power of the Holy Spirit at St Paul's. In the glorious love-permeated atmosphere of our Tuesday evening meetings, while a group of dedicated believers spent about half the evening in a side room praying for the power of Jesus to be seen and felt, they had found true hope, peace and joy in Him.

Some Christians seem to be suspicious or afraid of those who have been converted to Christianity from involvement in the occult. But these converts have often been in all kinds of spiritual trouble. They are people for whom Christ died. When they have found Him, they are frequently greatly gifted and extremely sincere in His service.

I have met many Christians who have told me hair-raising stories of how, before their conversion, they became demon-possessed through involvement with spiritism. One of these, Robert Lee, became my main helper in dealing with demonised people. He learned so much the hard way in his own attempts to become a medium. He wrote to me describing his horrible experiences:

"It was April 9th. I had a big job, a big salary, a big office and a big problem. I had been searching for God, but as I sat at my desk after lunch, I watched my hand pick up a pen and start to write. I didn't want to write. With an effort I could have stopped it for a time, but I didn't put forth that effort.

"My hand started to write out the name of my *guide*, or was it yet another *guide*. I was becoming confused. It was a very long name with a lot of letters, and half way through the spelling I was told we would finish writing it tomorrow. It sounds hilarious now, but it wasn't a bit funny then. I felt I just couldn't take any more.

"I had only snatches of sleep for two months. As I lay in bed, wide awake, whispering voices prepared me for the next ordeal to prove I was worthy of God. I had submitted myself to all these whispered preparations in night-after-night and day-after-day sessions, being told by a voice to go on some meaningless journey or talk to some particular person and *it would be all right.*

"It had not been all right at all. My colleagues were beginning to give me strange looks. I was fighting to remain normal at work and home. There was not only that voice but also clear coloured pictures like colour television in my mind. I saw them in a rectangular panel to the right of dead centre. My arms and hands were starting to do things I had not told them to do. I remember particularly the horror of even drinking a cup of tea. As soon as I decided to pick up the cup, it picked up itself and came at my mouth as my arm moved out of my control.

"All the wonderful promises the voices had made to me were just not worth it. I couldn't keep up the pace. Even as I thought this I knew *they* were hearing my thoughts.. 'God,' I murmured, 'I'm just no good to you. Let me go back to a normal life.'

"The answer to my pleas was dynamic. A force seized my shoulders and thrust me down onto my blotting pad. How long could I hold on? 'God,' I began weakly. But a voice inside my mind said, 'This isn't God . . . this is the devil.' The voice added, 'And now I'm going to drive you mad.'

"I could feel the thing inside me moving in for the kill. What an utter fool I had been. I had tried to find God outside the beloved Saviour Jesus Christ. This landed me in the hands of the devil – like a fly tied up in a spider's web.

"My wife and I had been investigating spiritism in which her family had some non-active interest. My wife soon realised I was getting deeply involved and urged me to take it more easily. Tuesdays I was at the spiritist church in Ilford for the 'healing' services. Sunday night I attended the worship service. But the big attraction was visiting mediums. I seemed to receive message after message from alleged parents and friends who had 'passed over.'

"Looking back, I should think ninety percent of the messages were so general as to be inept. For instance, 'I've got a kind old man wanting to speak to his son. That's you, sir, with the blue tie. He says you must not worry about mother. She is at peace and sends you all her love.' Folk still sorrowing for lost relatives often swallow this sort of thing, as I did. Ten percent of the messages I received, however, could not be easily explained. No doubt the devil has some genuine information to give to cause people to become further involved.

83

"I introduced the ouija board to my family and friends, even encouraging my children to participate. We got an active response with a lot of information, some of which could not have been faked easily, such as the name my father called my mother (Meg) which no one else knew but me.

"At this moment of reality I knew I had been deceived. Fragments of nearly forgotten Scripture came back to me and I knew I had separated myself from God in denying Jesus Christ. I knew I had sinned utterly. I had loved things which were an abomination to God. What possible hope could there be now?

"I got up and walked over to my office window. The thing inside me was moving up and down. It could influence my movements, thought and speech. It was like having another pair of hands on one's steering wheel. How could I fight it? Then the thought came to me of the night before and filled me with dread. My family had practically given me up. I just had to find help. But where? My doctor? He had been giving me loads of sleeping pills which had had little effect. I had refused to tell him why I couldn't sleep. A hospital? I could just imagine trying to explain!

"Suddenly I realised I was possessed. I remembered enough Scripture to convince me that I was demonised. The thing inside me actually reacted when I thought of demons. I asked myself, 'What is the opposite of the devil?' A church came to mind and I thought, 'I must find a church.' "

Robert Lee, my correspondent, did find a church and was completely delivered from this evil power through the effective exorcism ministry conducted by some Presbyterian ministers. After this, all traces of psychological and emotional disorder disappeared. He was a free man.

I had no part in Robert's problem or his deliverance which had taken place twelve years before I met him. The devil tries to mislead us but his power is limited. God is sovereign and the devil, in the end, serves God's purposes. So any attempt by Satan to sidetrack me into spiritism had the opposite effect. It opened my eyes to the main source of the problem of evil spirits in people's lives.

The majority of those who needed deliverance in my own ministry proved that beyond dispute. In nine out of every ten cases their problems began with occult, especially spiritist, involvement.

A woman from Southend kept hearing voices which would send her off by train to London, where she would wander the streets guided like a robot from place to place. She would be missing for days on end, and her husband was getting frantic with her odd behaviour. Her son, a Christian, was so concerned that he brought her along to St Paul's for deliverance. After prayer in the name of Jesus she was freed, and then able to resume a normal married life.

Another woman came to me absolutely terrified because she had developed automatic writing and other paranormal phenomena. She was also set free through believing prayer.

I was even summoned to a local school after three frightened schoolboys had told their headteacher that they had gone into a trance, and one had brandished a knife, threatening his schoolmate. Following the incident the headteacher, a Christian, phoned me and asked me to exorcise the boys, who had become violent following a seance. I quickly discovered that they had been dabbling in the game of ouija.

They told me that one of them believed he was a medium. He claimed to have seen his dead grandfather who told him to do evil things.

When the boys came round they couldn't remember exactly what had happened. In the name of Jesus they were gloriously delivered.

One of the most astonishing cases I dealt with in my early days at St Paul's was that of Olive, a woman who several times came to me for help, finally saying she wanted to escape from the "curse of the three demons."

She told me her trouble started in 1958 when her mother died.

"We were very, very close – almost telepathic," said Olive. "She died of cancer after a long, horrible illness."
Olive claimed that she was under great stress because of the death, and as she stood beside the coffin she felt very bitter towards God.

"It was then that I heard an evil laugh," she declared. "I didn't know what it was at the time. But I actually heard a horrible, horrible laugh."
She believed in Christ, but hadn't been to church for many years. Shortly after this she suddenly started dreaming of a man in black. She couldn't understand it.

She found a small prayer book and a Bible among her mother's belongings and one night, three or four weeks after her death, she was still so upset that she got up and burned them. She no longer believed in God.

Then Olive started to feel that someone was watching her . . . that something was there . . . even though she couldn't see anything.

One night it was so bad that she got up and went downstairs.

She sat in the dark and said: "Satan, if you are there let me see you." AND HE CAME. He actually appeared in a corner of the room.

He was dressed completely in black. He didn't have horns and a tail as she had thought, but was handsome, and very tall – his head almost touched the ceiling.

Like a zombie she sat there scared stiff, and eventually she told him she wanted proof he existed, whereupon he told her to go to an address in London. He spoke with a normal voice, laughed and disappeared. Olive recognised the laugh as the one she had heard at her mother's coffin.

After a few weeks she plucked up the courage to go to the address in London. A man answered the door and asked if she had come for the seance. She said "Yes," and decided to join in.

The seance was taken by a poker-faced Madam who spoke to Olive afterwards and asked her to go again. Olive told some friends about this, and they thought it was a great joke; they asked her to try and make contact with the devil. She tried – and succeeded.

Olive went into a trance and her "friends" told her afterwards that they had got messages through her. She started to see the Madam regularly and she was used to make contact with the devil. She didn't realise that she was getting more and more deeply involved. She was in a whirlpool and she was getting near to the point of no return.

Suddenly Olive found that she couldn't stand the Bible or a cross. In a frenzy she destroyed all the Bibles in the house. She has no recollection of doing it – but just found them torn up on the floor. One had been hidden, but in a trance she found it. It was a big thick Bible that she couldn't consciously have had the strength to tear to shreds. But she did.

She had a beautiful crucifix, but found it smashed – she had been so violent that she had broken a chair as well.

The coven used her constantly to get their messages through. Olive would go into a trance and was always seeing the devil. He used to speak and she would get directions what to do and what not to do . . . he controlled her.

She moved to another house and Fred, her husband, started going to church. Olive went to see a psychiatrist, and on her third visit he almost had her committed to a mental hospital, but could not make a real diagnosis in the realm of known mental illness.

Eventually she went to see a minister at the London Healing Mission. He came and exorcised the house, and kept repeating, "Jesus Christ, Jesus Christ." Olive went into a trance. She couldn't stand that Name.

The minister gave her a blessing, and when she came out of the trance she felt a little better. But two or three months later another Bible went. She always felt that the devil had the greatest power, so she gave up for a couple of years after that. Then she heard about what was happening at St Paul's, Hainault, and decided to go along.

She had very bad spinal trouble at the time. The pain was so severe that she would black out and the devil would come to her. She spent a couple of hundred pounds on osteopathic treatment, but it never improved.

At St Paul's the Tuesday meetings were small in those days, with only about 20 people attending. Someone introduced me to Olive, but she was hardly friendly.

"I've had enough of you ministers," she told me curtly.

The second time she came, she said, "I've dabbled in demonology and can't believe in Jesus. I talk to the devil. It's getting out of control." She paused, then she asked, "Can you help me to be free of this evil?"

I thought her rather strange and took what she said only half seriously. "Come along to our healing service," I said.

The third time she came to church, she spotted a stack of Bibles near the door and felt drawn to them. She had an overwhelming feeling that if she stayed she would start to tear up the Bibles, so she walked out.

Later Olive came to see me. We had a good talk, but I was still very new in this ministry and didn't really understand what I was up against.

Olive and her husband came to St Paul's a couple more times on Sundays. One time she went into a trance while everyone was praying. Her husband called me over and I tried to anoint her with oil, according to the pattern of the letter of James (Chap. 5, v 14).

That was the worst thing I could have done, and she began to fight me. When she came round I took her to the vicarage, but she felt a sudden fear of me and said she couldn't bear me near her.

At a subsequent meeting she again went into a trance and, once again, I had to take her out of the meeting and into the vicarage.

I prayed for her as she was in these trances and each time it was a mighty struggle. Although this was all still very new to me, I knew I had to take authority through the power of Jesus.

"I'm witchcraft I'm witchcraft!" a voice vaguely recognisable as hers shouted during a service. Then it squeaked, "She's mine! She's mine! She's mine! You can't have her. I possess her. Who are you? Who are you? Who are you?"

"I'm Trevor Dearing," I replied.

"I'll destroy you. I'm not afraid of you," came the reply as this incredible conversation continued. But I was gaining more confidence.

"I come in the name of Jesus to cast you out!" I said loudly and firmly.

"Have mercy! Have mercy! I'm frightened of Jesus," the voice admitted (Mark 1: 23-26).

I was thoroughly convinced there was only one way out of this situation. With complete faith in the power of God and with no doubt about the outcome, I performed my first exorcism.

"I take authority over you in the name of Jesus. You will not hurt this woman or anyone else any more. Out! Out!" I shouted. "Go!"

As happened with other demons that I later exorcised from her, it left with a blood-curdling scream.

"It's gone! It's gone!" Olive cried with relief as I consoled a frightened congregation.

On one occasion in her home a demon came out of her, but it entered her dog. The poor thing lay on his back with his legs in the air, and was shaking all over. I prayed over him and he has been all right since.

Then Olive found that she had a terrible attack of pain in her back, and her husband asked me to go and pray for her.

I laid my hands on Olive's head while she was blacked out and tried to relieve the condition. She came round, began to move her legs, and there was no pain. She stood up. That was the first time in 14 years that she had walked free of pain.

She asked Fred to buy her a Bible and I wrote a scripture verse on the flyleaf. Three weeks later the Bible was in shreds.

"That's it," she said. "I'm not going to fight the devil any more."

But she did – and another Bible went. The pain came back, and one of her legs lost all feeling, so that she could actually stick pins in it and not feel a thing.

Olive started coming back to the Tuesday healing sessions and, after four months, her back was completely cured.

I then concentrated on trying to bring her leg back to life. Some months later, as I laid hands on her, the pain was so unbearable that she had to sit down. Then the pain just went, as she sat there, and did not return. She had been dragging that leg for two years.

The coven, however, heard that Olive was turning to the Lord, and one day a man called at her house. "Your group want you back," he said on the doorstep. She told him she would not go back. But he returned a few days later with a frightening threat.

"The coven has cursed you with the CURSE OF THE THREE DEMONS and you will die after six months," he said menacingly.

Olive was terrified, because the coven had used the curse on three different occasions while she was a member, and all three people had died.

The "Curse of the three demons" lasts six months. First the person is taken over by the demon of "Fear", then by the demon of "Despair"; then by the demon of "Death".

Shortly afterwards she was at a Tuesday meeting when she went into a trance; she then almost strangled her husband.

As he gurgled and gasped for breath, I stopped her in the name of the Lord and got the demon out. Her hands relaxed from around his neck and she sat down, not knowing what she had just done.

Three months later I prayed out the demon of "Fear".

Soon afterwards the evil man returned and told her the exact date of her death – September 16th.

This was a Sunday, and she and her husband came to church. Olive had until evening to live if the curse was to come true. I knew about it as she came forward for this last desperate battle.

There was a mighty struggle as I cast out the demon. She was blaspheming and cursing Christ. I then conversed with the demon and commanded it out in the name of Jesus. Like the others it came out with a horrible scream.

Olive suddenly got a terrific pain in the heart and went into a sea of blackness. Many, including Anne, unable to feel a pulse, thought she had died. I then came and removed two more demons – "despair" and "death". Over the months of terrible struggle, I had cast twelve demons out of her soul.

The delivered woman later told her story to the newspaper, the Southend Echo. She told a reporter:

"I felt marvellous afterwards. I just felt free. I had not felt like that before. Since then . . . nothing. I am free.

"I'm now a complete Christian. I have been blessed by the Holy Spirit and am very happy. I am also free from pain and worries."

Olive learned how to stand her ground against all Satan's attempts to repossess her. The victory had been won in the name of the Lord Jesus Christ, who conquered all the powers of darkness including Satan himself, when He cried, "It is finished!" on the cross of Calvary. Jesus rose from the dead and shattered all the minions of hell as He ascended to glory. He is "far above all principalities and powers and every name that can be named, not only in this world, but that which is to come."

Another incident which Trevor remembers well was the exorcism of a 28-year-old woman whom the "News of the World" singled out for special mention, as she wore a very short miniskirt, a scant blouse, and had an intense sexual problem. Trevor writes:

"I suspected she was demon possessed when she got out of the doctor's car – he had brought her to me for help. But she declared loudly that she would not go near me as I was 'too powerful'.

"We eventually got her into the church. There was no one else there but the Christian doctor and my wife. The girl first locked herself in the lavatory, and when she came out she became delirious and started rolling under the pews crying out: 'I'm a demon of seduction.'

"The doctor had to chase after her. I managed to pray for her and finally God drove the demon out."

# The power of voodoo broken

*Trevor also well remembers having to deal with voodoo:*

"Marina, a heavily-built West Indian woman, had had a terrifying shock when she discovered a cockerel's head, with horrible protuberant eyes, staring up at her from the dining table of her home in London. For she knew at that moment that a voodoo curse had been put on her and her house.

"The terror of the chilling curse made her shake uncontrollably with fear. Her eyes rolled and her face twitched, for she was afraid she would soon be dead. For two years she was tormented in horrible, indescribable ways, unable to cope with her job as a teacher of handicapped children.

"Then the voodoo terrors began to grip her even tighter, and the frightening hallucinations that she had been having became worse. Fear often drove her to violence and once, under the power of the curse, she nearly throttled two Pentecostal pastors who were trying to exorcise her. They were only saved when one of them struggled free from her grip and was able to grab a phone and dial 999 for police help. They took the struggling Marina off to a mental hospital, and there the powerful woman was often uncontrollable.

"I first met Marina at St Paul's, when she came along for help. I immediately sensed a voodoo curse and knew that there would have to be a fantastic battle before she could be free. Voodoo is a system of magic worship practised by Negroes and Creoles, and once a curse is put on someone, that can mean the end of their sanity, and even their life.

"And this spell nearly spelled the end of my life – for as I began to pray for this huge lady, her giant hands went for my throat. Stewards came dashing forward and did what they could to restrain her, but it was the power of Jesus that held those hideous demonic forces at bay as I began to cast out the voodoo spirit. For ten horrifying minutes the battle raged, and eventually, as the sweat poured down her face, the evil spirit left her and she was free. Glory be to Jesus!

"The change that came over her was amazing. She began to grin, beaming a real love towards me and the praising congregation. She had been transformed in those minutes by Jesus, the great deliverer, but strangely she remembered nothing of the deadly combat that had taken place in releasing her."

Marina, who is now a committed Christian, was soon back teaching handicapped children – in her right mind – and became a powerful witness for Christ.

✳ ✳ ✳ ✳ ✳ ✳ ✳ ✳ ✳ ✳ ✳

# Birmingham

Anne recalls: "One Sunday evening some years ago when Trevor was due to take a meeting at Birmingham Christian Centre, we received a phone call before the service about a young man who was epileptic, who would be coming for ministry. So we arrived a little earlier, and the young man came into the vestry. I guessed he was about twenty.

"He explained how he had been in an accident a few years before and his spine had been very badly damaged, and that he had then had these epileptic attacks. Trevor had asked me if I would be all right with this young man, as he was tall, and heavier than I was, for the service was about to begin. I assured him that I would, so he went out of the vestry, leaving me with the young man.

"I discerned that there was an evil spirit within him. I am not one who sees evil spirits everywhere, but on this occasion I said to the young man:

" 'I discern that at some time an evil spirit has entered your body, and I'm going to cast it out.'

"I rebuked the spirit and told it to get out of this young man's life and never to make another entry, and I told him that he was going to be better.

"He was sitting on a chair at the time, and he fell off the chair at my feet. He was crying out, and frothing at the mouth. Then he had an attack of rather violent coughing, and he said, 'Something is leaving my stomach, I can feel it leaving.'

"I said to him, 'It's all right, it's going now. Don't hurry; I've got all evening. I can stay here for as long as you need me.'

"When he was able, I helped him rise to his feet and he sat down again. 'Oh,' he said, 'what a load has been lifted out of my system! I felt it coming up after I had that coughing attack.'

"A month later his mother telephoned to say how well he was, and that he'd been able to take himself on a continental holiday. Some time after that it was confirmed that he was doing wonderfully well."

Some of the happenings that our congregations experienced during services were unexpectedly hair-raising. Like the time when, as I began preaching, a young man in his teens suddenly let out a howl like a werewolf and started running backwards and forwards at the rear of the church. He had his teeth bared, and gave the impression that he would have bitten me if he could.

A shiver went through the congregation as stewards pounced and tried to grab him. I discovered later that he had been having horrific nightmares, going into trances and having violent outbursts. He had once drawn a knife on a friend. He said also he even felt "something" urging him to commit suicide.

In the name of Jesus I took control of the situation and addressed the spirits in the "werewolf" who cried out from within him. I told them their reign of terror had ended, and bound them. Then I cast them forth in the name of Jesus.

He fell to the floor and then, just as suddenly, sprang to his feet and shouted: "Praise the Lord for all He has done!" It was astonishing. We all rejoiced at the transformation.

There were many cases of people beginning to scream out uncontrollably as we ministered to them (Acts 8: 7). In one case a teenage girl had to be taken from the main service and into a vestry which became a battleground until midnight.

Trevor recollects:
"Demon after demon called out its name before being cast out of this young life. The demons argued with me, saying such things as, 'Christ died for people like you but He didn't die for creatures like us.'

"A powerful demon told me that it had entered the girl when she was born. After being freed from her tormentors, the girl told me she had been dreadfully deprived as a child. She had spent most of her life in an orphanage. Later I learned from a psychiatrist that she had always shown marked signs of maladjustment. He gave me a very poor forecast for her future. But after the deliverance ministry, counselling and rehabilitation in a Christian family unit she became emotionally stable, successful at school and is now living a normal life.

"In view of these successes in the name of Jesus, I asked myself, 'Is this exorcism associated with one particular place – St Paul's Church, Hainault?'

"The question was answered when invitations came to conduct missions all over England. To my surprise, I met similar manifestations in other places (Acts 5: 16). One of these occurred at Evensong in a parish church in Sheffield. As I began to pray, a man jumped up in the front pew and started screaming at me. He waved his arms ferociously.

"As I took a step towards him he fled up the aisle, pursued by sidesmen. They caught him in the churchyard and managed to escort him to the porch. I proceeded to give him deliverance ministry as he became more and more violent. Finally he seemed to vomit, something intangible coming out of his mouth. Then he walked triumphantly back into the church crying out, 'I'm free! I'm free! I'm free!' I understand he later pursued a university course and attained a law degree."

In another town, by arrangement with the vicar, and by permission of the bishop, we actually held a special deliverance service for a young woman. She had been so involved in occultism and the drug scene that she had a black cross tattooed upside down upon her back. A sympathetic doctor had gone to great trouble to have it removed when she became a Christian. Nevertheless, she still reacted violently to the name of Jesus and especially to the elements of bread and wine at Holy Communion.

She still needed deliverance ministry, in spite of wanting to be a Christian. After the ministry of the delivering word she was able to praise the Lord and partake of the sacrament for the first time.

There was another remarkable incident one night when I arrived home to find a sturdy, rough-looking Cockney standing on my doorstep. He was shaking like a leaf. With him were two equally-built men, looking very agitated.

"Can you help my friend?" The question seemed to explode from one of the men's lips. He added, "He has attacked his wife and might kill her unless you can do something for him. Something must be done tonight."

Slowly the story unfolded. A fortnight previously, while his wife was on night duty as a nurse, the man had been alone and felt somewhat bored. He decided to play ouija to see if there was anything in it. To his horror voices began to pound through his brain and eventually one spirit began to take control of his actions. He became violent, and when his wife came home he attacked her. Since then he had been unable to work and was in a terrible emotional state. He was desperate to find relief from voices and visions. He was not a churchgoer or in any way religious and had not seen a doctor for years. He had no history of psychiatric disorder.

There was only one thing to do. I gave him deliverance ministry in the name of Jesus Christ, casting out three evil spirits. Like others during this ministry, as in the days of Jesus, he became "as one dead", lying at my feet (Mark 9: 26). Eventually he rose a free man.

It is not only spiritism, however, that can open the door to demon possession. The meditational exercises of yoga are similarly dangerous. A young man who had been deeply involved in these practices disrupted a mission meeting in the Midlands. There was a terrible noise of furniture being smashed at the rear of the church. He was picking up chairs and crashing them one against the other.

The minister and stewards tried to restrain him by pinning him to the floor. He shook them off with supernatural strength and ran from the building. Immediately I urged the congregation to pray.

"Destructive spirit, I bind you," I declared across the distance. "You shall not hurt him any more. In the name of Jesus, I loose him from your control."

We then prayed that the Holy Spirit would direct his feet back to the church.

Sure enough, he returned. He explained about the yoga meditation, which had obviously been the point of the spirit's entry. "I felt my body was going one way, despite all my mind wanted to do. I was taken over by something that used my body."

It was all over in two minutes. He renounced the practice from the heart and, at the word of command, yet another spirit was dispatched to the pit to await the judgement of Christ.

Exorcism ministry needs a special gift – the *discerning of spirits*. This is the God-given ability to feel the presence of God or the presence of evil in something that is said, or to feel the presence of evil in people or places. The gift of discernment has not only been needed to expose genuine demon possession, but also to help those who have been suffering from pseudo-possession.

A number of people who have come to us thinking they were possessed were found to be mistaken. Some of them were suffering from neurosis. These unfortunate people can unwittingly draw energy from Christians who abortively try to exorcise them. Obviously such ministry does not help such people. The ultimate source of their trouble lies elsewhere. They must be pointed lovingly to their real need in order to be genuinely healed.

Discernment is especially needed in cases of mental illness. Those of us who believe in the reality of evil spirits must recognise that a person's mind can become sick as well as his soul or spirit (see *Total Healing*). To treat all fears, depressions or abnormal mental conditions as possession by evil spirits is devastatingly wrong. In fact, it can cause terrible damage to sensitive people. In my ministry I have met several people whose minds have been badly shaken by such treatment at the hands of would-be exorcists. It has taken some time to restore them to an even keel, both emotionally and spiritually. One such person was Mavis.

This young lady was a chronic depressive with a tragic history of rejection, failure and hurt. Her hopes of a fulfilling life had been constantly dashed and she suffered also from several physical incapacities which deeply affected her life. She was a very sensitive person, deeply committed as a Christian but quite terrified of disobeying or failing God.

Church people had tried to help Mavis, treating her as a case for deliverance ministry. At one time she was subjected to two and a half hours of unremitting exorcism during which she became hysterical, violent and abusive. These reactions had been treated as additional demons to be cast out. Battered and bewildered, she turned to me in the hope that discernment would be forthcoming.

I ministered healing of the memories, a treatment of long duration and taking several sessions in which sins, traumatic experiences and fears are laid open to the healing balm of the Holy Spirit. She is completely healed today.

The clearest test that can be employed in seeking to discover whether a person is suffering some psychosomatic disorder or is demonised, is to find out whether the person has been in some way involved with the occult. Although the Lord gives me the gift of discernment, there was a case of one particular man who implored my help, because he was in desperate need.

His behaviour had become uncontrollable; he felt urged to shout out blasphemy in Christian meetings; was hearing voices, and seeing frightening visions. I enquired and discovered that the trouble began with his trying to become a medium twenty years previously. I felt he was possessed. But I found strong resistance to the power of Jesus on the part of the demons, who would not obey my commands to manifest themselves.

"Could I be wrong in my discernment?" I asked myself. I sought the cooperation of the possessed man by urging him to say, "The blood of Jesus cleanses me from all sin." At this there was an intense reaction by the demons with cries of "No! No! We possess him."

Three spirits left him after deliverance ministry. In the end he could shout the words about the blood of Jesus. He knew he was a free man.

This man had been receiving psychiatric and other medical help for many years. However, it was my privilege through the power of discernment to expose his real enemy and effectively deal with it. Such ministry in the name of Jesus is miraculous.

*       *       *       *       *       *       *

Exorcism without a doubt is the most controversial part of Trevor's ministry, but he remembers a time when he strongly opposed it:

"Like many today, I felt it was a thing of the Dark Ages. Like witch-burning and slave markets, it didn't happen any more. It was putting the clock back to the Middle Ages and was misleading vulnerable and dependent people.

"I can well remember being questioned along the lines of my possible naive acceptance of the Scriptures at my interview for the R.E. post at a Harlow comprehensive school. I said then that my conclusion was that all unscientific Biblical material had to be transposed into the more obvious thought forms of our modern society. It meant that our belief about demonology would be reinterpreted into the psychological terms of which my academic training had given me a good working knowledge.

"But after I was baptised in the Holy Spirit, I, like all those who have had the same experience, had my eyes opened to the reality of the supernatural in Christianity – not only in theology, but also in experience. And it is to be remembered that one of the gifts of the Holy Spirit is that of the discerning of spirits.

"The baptism of the Spirit not only opens one's eyes to the reality and experience of the supernatural endowment of the Holy Spirit in His miraculous abilities, but also to the reality of those 'principalities and powers, spiritual hosts of wickedness in high places' of which the apostle Paul speaks in Ephesians 6, and, of vital importance, the victory of Christ over them.

"Since my ministry began, oppressed, possessed and afflicted people have found complete deliverance. I have cast out voodoo, psychic, addictive, witchcraft, unclean, tormenting, seductive, suicidal, religious (yes, religious), depressive, fearful and other spirits, from the lives of men and women of all ages.

"I have even ministered to disturbed children who have needed exorcism. This has usually been done while they have been asleep, because otherwise it might have terrified them. I often get the parent to hold the sleeping child who has manifested evidence of demon possession, in their arms, while I cast out the evil spirit."

Jesus is victorious and His power is still the same today as in Bible days to work such miracles of deliverance.

# Part Three

Miracles through
answered prayer

# 6

# God's use of the
# ministry of intercession

We have always taught that, although it is the norm for sick people to receive direct ministry from Anne and myself in the name of Jesus, yet it is right for us to encourage Christians to come to Jesus on behalf of sick relatives and friends for whom they are deeply concerned, and to believe that He only has to speak the word of healing from His heavenly throne, and their loved ones will be healed. So we have taught petitioners not only to pray to Jesus for loved ones, but to **believe** for a miracle.

To this end we brought into being an Intercessors' Fellowship to go alongside our ministry to the sick. It was led, until her retirement, by Mrs Stella Godsmark, who lives at Spilsby. We had about forty intercessors to whom she sent prayer requests, giving them as much detail as possible about each sufferer, including age, sex, address, and especially informing them about as much as was known of each sick person's condition and need.

Stella split the Fellowship into groups so that no one would have too many folk for whom to intercede, but could concentrate on a few. She urged the intercessors to engage in believing prayer and to have real faith in God for victorious answers. She regularly encouraged them by sending out testimonies to the answers to their faith, and always sent me a copy in response to the prayer-requests I had sent her. It is difficult to exaggerate the number of the miracles that happened all over the nation in answer to our Fellowship's faith-full (*i.e.* full of faith!) petitions.

These included healings of or provision for:

- cancer
- broken bones
- broken relationships
- the salvation of loved ones
- depression
- phobias
- chest conditions
- pain
- jobs for unemployed people
- new homes
- blood pressure
- organic illness

and so on, to include just about every imaginable need. Stella had a remarkable, God-given calling and effectiveness in this ministry.

Sometimes during our services people received the laying-on of hands on behalf of absent friends or relatives. This is healing by proxy. We asked whoever was receiving the ministry to concentrate in faith and love, and believe for the person who was sick. We remembered that, in the Scripture, people came to Jesus for their absent loved ones, and how He said, ' "It will be done *just as you believed* it would." And his servant was healed at that very hour.'

105

Another feature of our Tuesday evening meetings at St Paul's, Hainault was what we called the Ten O'Clock Link Up. At ten o'clock precisely we would pray for the absent sick. We actually encouraged people to send in prayer requests, which we, together with the faith-filled con-gregation, brought before the Lord at 10.00 pm each Tuesday.

We had asked petitioners to sit quietly and spiritually "tune in with us" in their homes at this time. People would call out the names of friends and loved ones who needed believing prayer. Trevor would then pray, asserting the power and control of God over every situation and over every sickness. He urged the congregation not simply to pray for friends but actually *believe* for them.

There were many great miracles that took place as a result of this time. A young married woman with two children wrote, saying:

"I am writing to tell you of the wonderful progress my mother has made, since having been prayed for during the Ten O'Clock Link Up. She stood up by herself at that very moment. She is now back home, and the nurses are amazed that she could stand up and walk after such a serious illness resulting from a fall."

We have received many letters like this thanking God and giving glory to Jesus.

An answer to prayer through the Link Up which was an emotional experience for Anne and Trevor took place hours before Anne's stepfather, Len Ford, was due to have his right foot amputated. Len, a retired bus driver, had found himself crippled up with pain from blood clots in both his legs. One cleared up with hospital treatment, but the other did not, and gangrene was setting in. One Tuesday, the night before the operation was due to take place, Trevor prayed during the Link Up for a miracle, and without their knowing until the next day, the blood immediately began flowing into his right foot.

Next morning the surgeon came to see Len and had to blink when he saw the doomed right foot was a healthy pink.

"This is remarkable," he said, scratching his head. "Do you believe in miracles Mr Ford? Well, as long as you live, remember you have got a miracle right foot."

Since 1975, except for two years pastoring St Luke's Episcopal Church, Seattle, USA, Anne and I have had no church base for our ministry. We have been entirely engaged in itinerant work, mainly at public meetings. Stella Godsmark's retirement from her work as secretary and organiser of the Intercessors' Fellowship resulted in the work never quite getting off the ground since that time, although we pass on to our friends who receive our newsletter the names of those who need intercessory prayer, and miracles of healing continue to occur.

However, Anne and I have still felt a burden to give people at meetings the opportunity to bring their needy but absent loved ones to the Lord. I have done this by asking those who desired to be involved in this spiritual act of faith, to stand and in silence think about and also picture these absent folk in real love and to sympathise (suffer with) with the ones they have on their hearts. After a little while I ask them to turn their thoughts to Jesus and visualise Him on His throne in glory. I have reminded them that He said, after His resurrection, "All authority in heaven and on earth has been given to me." (Matt. 28) Then I have suggested that they speak aloud the name of their loved one to Him. I wait a while, then I say, "On the count of three shout out the Name 'Jesus' and believe for a miracle across the miles." The cry has often echoed around the building. After this I urge them to praise the Lord in anticipation of good news. The results of this act of faith have come back to us by the score.

In Finland relatives had been urgently called to the hospital where their loved one was nearing the end with terminal cancer. They had gone to be with her when she died. However, miles away in Helsinki, another relative had taken a different course. She was standing in one of our meetings, believing Jesus for a miracle. The critically ill woman began to make an astonishing and rapid recovery. When we met Finnish friends later at a conference, they told us that the woman is now living a normal life, with no trace of cancer in her body.

On another occasion, in Ireland, I was given rather a shock during this ministry. As I was uttering the words about the healing of the absent sick, one intercessor suddenly fell with a tremendous crash onto the stone floor of the church. Angels must have hurried to put an invisible cushion under her, for she was not hurt. Her friend, however, who had been haemorrhaging, was **healed**. Florence later wrote:

"As I stood in the prayer line, thinking of her and what Jesus can do, the Lord touched me, and I fell down with a terrible bang in the Spirit. Well, since then, she has phoned to say that the bleeding has stopped and she hasn't taken a tablet since. We have praised the Lord in tears and laughter."

In this ministry the Lord has overcome all language barriers. He **had** to do so when we were in Spain. A remarkable miracle resulted. It involved a very sick woman on the other side of the country who didn't even know that faith was being exercised on her behalf at a meeting we were holding in a believer's house.

I learned the next day that this very sick woman just couldn't understand what was happening to her as she lay in bed. All she knew was that at about 10.00 pm she began to feel very much better. She could hardly believe it, but as strength flowed into her body and new life into her limbs, she decided to see if she could get out of bed. She easily succeeded, and was discovered, early in the morning, to be doing her housework – for the first time in ten years! Excited relatives asked us if we could go and visit her. We did so, and told her that it was Jesus who had made her whole.

Sometimes believers have actually asked me, during a prayer time for the absent sick, to *minister* to them as they have believed for an absent sick person who was on their heart. One woman wrote:

"About eleven years ago I went to a Service in the Millmead Centre at Guildford where you were speaking. My friend was ill, she was expecting her fourth child and had been very sick for five months. She was weak and in bed most of the time. I came forward for prayer on her behalf. That night her sickness stopped, she became stronger and a normal healthy son 'Danny' was born."

His parents became Christians through this experience.

One final way in which God brings healing to the absent sick remains to be discussed. This is the way in which believers can take prayer cloths which have been prayed over by a Spirit-anointed minister of God to a sick loved one, to be used as yet another 'point of contact' between the healing power of God and the afflicted person. This ministry is based on the account in Acts (Chapter 19) which reads:

*God did extraordinary miracles through Paul. Handkerchiefs and aprons that had touched him were taken to the sick and their illnesses were cured and the evil spirits left them..*

(verses 11-12)

109

We have not particularly promulgated this ministry, but when asked to do so, have prayed over handkerchiefs or pieces of cloth at the request of believers, and we have received testimony to some "extraordinary" miracles.

A few typical letters are:

- "I feel I must write. I've been an arthritic for a number of years, with other troubles. Now I have received a tremendous improvement over the last few weeks after receiving a prayer-cloth. Now the fear of being alone that I have suffered the last twelve months has gone!"

- "Just to thank you for the prayer cloth that you kindly sent. I am glad to say that the ulcer in my left leg has been healed."

- "I wrote to you about my mother Mrs Xigi, who lives in Greece and was suffering from cancer. I sent her the prayer cloth you sent me and I am happy to tell you that by the grace of the Lord she is better. The lump has completely gone."

- "I have to testify to healing and help we have been receiving through prayer, belief and the use of the prayer handkerchief. My wife's blood pressure continues to be normal."

When people request a prayer cloth, the whole emphasis in my instructions is that it is Jesus alone who heals. I urge the sufferers to read the gospel story and put their faith in the risen Christ. I urge them also to confess their sins to Him and take Him as their Saviour before using the cloth. I suggest that they place the cloth, if possible, on the affected part, and command the sickness to go in the name of Jesus. I instruct them to give thanks to Him for what He has done. The fact that this message has been received is shown by the following letter:

> I was thrilled to receive a prayer cloth as I've heard about them. I know there is no magic in it but it is an aid to faith. I used my prayer cloth doing all the things you told me. I put my cloth on my chest and rebuked the enemy. I kept the cloth next to my chest, inside my clothes. Jesus gave me strength and healing.

During the 1970s, when the local and national press were showing a keen interest in what was happening at St Paul's, Hainault, the News of the World decided to investigate the case of Yvonne Perry, whose doctors had told her mother: "She will need a miracle if she is to live."

Yvonne was being treated for a rare and serious blood disease. A slight cut would have meant she could bleed to death.

Mrs Perry told the News of the World: "I went to see Mr Dearing and we prayed together. He told me, 'Your daught-er is healed. Don't pray so hard now, something is on the way.' "

Mrs Perry added that doctors were astonished when they next saw Yvonne. She was cured.

# Mrs G. O., Tamworth:

"I'm writing to say thank you for praying for me. I wrote some time ago about both my legs – they kept going ulcerated. Well, praise God, through your healing prayers my legs have healed."

# Miss L. B., Belle Vale:

"In October I wrote to you asking for your prayers as I was going into hospital for biopsy of both breasts. Praise be to God I went to hospital for a last check-up the other week, and I was told by doctors that they had removed a lump under a nipple, but that it was benign, and that everything was alright. Thank you for prayers."

# Mrs M. R. wrote:

"My friend Muriel, who is often on Stella Godsmark's prayer list that she sends out, wrote to me and said she was healed of epilepsy at one of your meetings recently."

# Prescot, Merseyside: heroin addiction

Tony had been a heroin addict for twenty years, and a consequence of his addiction was cirrhosis of the liver. He had started some new treatment that was causing him some horrendous side-effects. On the Sunday of a weekend when we were missioning on Merseyside he was treated all day long at the hospital for an embolism in his leg. He was told that he would have to stop the treatment and was asked to return for a scan and be seen by a consultant the next day.

We were informed on the telephone and prayed. Tony had his scan and also a test on his liver. He was told that the embolism had disappeared and that his liver was functioning normally. The doctors could offer no explanation. Praise the Lord!

# R.W., Everton, Nr Lymington

"In early June I telephoned you and informed you that my Mother had just been told that she had stomach cancer. As you can imagine we were all in shock. I asked that you pray for her.

"I felt I should write and say thank you for your prayers. The nausea has gone; the pain in the chest has gone and also the pain in the back. She is now eating solid food again and is nearly back to her old self. The District Nurse said to me, 'It's magic!' We know it's not, and give all the thanks to God."

# Rayleigh, Essex

A minister living in Rayleigh wrote:

"I was rushed into Southend hospital as an emergency. I had not passed any water or motion for 4 days, X-rays showing that I had a tumour in the rectum, and it was a massive one, blocking everything. I was transferred to St Barts hospital, and further X-rays and scanning showed I also had a cordoma on the end of the spine, preventing me from passing anything that end, as well.

"Two specialists and two doctors considered it was not worth while operating, I was too far gone; the prospects of recovery were nil. One surgeon remarked, 'Well, let's have a go and experiment — there's nothing to lose; he won't make it.'

"But I was being prayed for!

"Two weeks later they came to the conclusion that I might make it after all. The cordoma had to be burned off with a laser beam and radio therapy, which took 6 weeks. They could not operate on the tumour, it was too near the spine.

"So the Lord took a hand. During one night He caused the tumour to break, and it discharged for many months, even after I left hospital. I finished up with a colostomy and a leg catheter. When I left the hospital, the surgeon, the doctor and the ward sister came to me and were lost for words. All they could say was, 'Not one of us here thought we would see you walk out of this hospital. It's a miracle; we don't understand it.' "

So, by one means or another we have seen that it is God's perfect will to heal physical afflictions, even of those who cannot receive direct, personal ministry, and we are without doubt that He does so.

# *Part Four*

## Miracles of changed lives

# 7

## God's use of the ministry of preaching

### A changed family

Trevor remembers: Before Anne and I were married, we faced the prospect of a long wait. At that time the rules of the Methodist Church prohibited a man studying for the ministry from getting married until he had undergone all his training and had been ordained. In my case this would mean a wait of almost seven years.

I had to go and minister for one year as a "lay student-pastor" in a rural Methodist circuit of churches in Norfolk, whilst Anne was training to be a nurse at a hospital in Retford.

I arrived at Melton Constable in Norfolk to begin my work there, in charge of ten small village churches, in September 1954, just before my twenty-first birthday. Lodgings had been found for me with two elderly but deeply Christian spinsters; and so my first task as a pastor in the Aylsham, Briston, Reepham Circuit began.

In order to pass my examinations for entry into a Methodist Theological College I would have to do a great deal of studying, and yet I had considerable responsibility, for a young man of my age, in ministering to the godly Methodist people who in small numbers attended those scattered churches. I went to serve these people with all the Bible-believing, evangelistic enthusiasm I had entered into at Cliff College. I would, I thought, minister all the truth I had recently learned. A test of its veracity would surely be: would it bear fruit in a rural Methodist circuit?

I had no sooner arrived there when Anne wrote with a very pleasant surprise — she was leaving Retford to nurse in Norfolk, eventually to work at Kelling Sanatorium, near Holt — only five miles from Melton Constable..

It was still not always easy for us to meet with one another owing to our lack of transportation and our respective duties, but it was certainly better than either of us had once expected, and we were able sometimes to serve the Lord together in those rural churches, as we met with the Lord's people.

Often I had to cycle twenty miles on totally dark roads to minister in those churches, but nothing could dampen my evangelistic enthusiasm. I even invited two Cliff College evangelists to conduct a ten-day mission in my two churches at Briston, and was delighted with the result: three people gave their hearts to the Lord. I started a "Christian Endeavour" group and encouraged Bible study and prayer meetings, which were attended by at least a few of the believers.

Our time in Norfolk was memorable in many ways, but especially for the conversion of a young married woman called Rosemary. It was remarkable from several points of view. I first met Rosemary in very unusual circumstances.

One Sunday morning I was preaching at Hall Street Methodist Church in Briston. My subject was the call and conversion of Peter the fisherman (Matthew 4: 18-22). I had finished the service, and when I walked out of the church into the porch, I was startled to find a woman there who was sobbing almost uncontrollably.

"What's the matter?" I asked in concern.

"I'm too unclean to come into Church," replied Rosemary, trying to suppress her sobs. "I've had an illegitimate child by a man other than my husband, and the Vicar says I and my child are spiritually dirty, and he won't baptise my baby. But I've been listening to your sermon through the cracks in the door. I heard every word you said, and I wish I could know Jesus as my Saviour and Lord."

"You can know Him now," I urged. "If only you ask Him into your heart and life by saying a simple prayer."

I then led Rosemary in the "Sinner's Prayer", acknowledging sin, repenting of it and asking Jesus to be her Saviour.

As I was reflecting that we are all dirty in the eyes of our holy God unless we have been cleansed through faith in what He did for us on Calvary, Rosemary said:

"I feel a deep peace filling my whole being. I feel I really do know Jesus now, in a personal way — it's wonderful! I believe He has taken away all my sins: I've got real peace with God, now."

"Yes, Jesus is wonderful!" I agreed.

"Would you be kind enough to come and pay us a visit, please?" she asked. "My husband's an alcoholic — he gets into terrible tempers when he's been drinking; it's awful — he shouts and raves at me and the children, and knocks me about if I don't keep out of his way. He scares us to death when he's like that.

"If only he could come to know the Lord, as I've done. What a difference it could make to us all!"

118

I made one or two tactful enquiries about the family from Christians in the neighbourhood and learned that the rows and arguments, screams and shouting which came through the doors and windows were indeed well known in the area.

When I later visited the home as I had promised, I found a most remarkable willingness on the part of the husband, Bob, to listen to the Gospel.

"I've seen such a change in my wife," he explained, "there must be something in it. She's suffered terribly with her nerves in the past, and now she seems so peaceful and well; please explain what has happened to her."

He accepted Jesus as his Lord and Saviour at that first visit, and soon began to testify to his workmates about what Jesus had done for him, especially the fact that he had been completely delivered from alcoholism.

Weeks later, when I was paying yet another visit to the home, I was met at the front gate by one of Rosemary and Bob's children, a boy who was about five years of age.

"Hallo Pastor Dearing," was his greeting. Then, pointing towards the front door, he said, "It's different in there! It's different in there! You see, we're very happy now. Jesus has come to live in our house and it's different in there."

People in the neighbourhood also expressed their surprise at the wonderful change that had taken place in that home, which was now a home of peace and love. It was the first instance we had witnessed of the way in which Jesus can transform marriages and homes, in fact the whole domestic scene, when He is invited into the situation.

For ourselves, despite all the other miracles we have witnessed, there is none greater than that of the changed and transformed life. It is usually God's use of the preaching of the Gospel — the good news of the possibility of coming into a personal relationship with God, through belief in His Son Jesus Christ, wherein this change begins. This chapter presents a small selection of instances where people have written to tell us about this wonderful change.

Jesus said that the change brought about is so radical that it can be described as "being born again" or "anew". Paul later put it in the words, "if anyone is in Christ, he is a new creation." The moment when we enter into a living relationship with God, He by His Holy Spirit indwells our lives, and "nothing is impossible with God" especially in the realm of the transformation of one's whole life. It becomes the first day in the rest of our lives. We view life, our own included, from an entirely different perspective and begin to live in a new dimension.

In His words: *"This is eternal life"* [life with a capital L] *"that they may know You, the only true God, and Jesus Christ, whom You have sent"*. (John 17: 3) [Brackets mine.]

✤ ✤ ✤ ✤ ✤ ✤ ✤ ✤ ✤ ✤ ✤ ✤ ✤ ✤ ✤ ✤ ✤ ✤ ✤ ✤ ✤ ✤ ✤ ✤

# Well and truly blessed

My husband David and I would like to encourage you by telling you what a wonderful blessing you have been to us since we gave our lives to the Lord eighteen months ago. We both became Christians during Mission to London at Q.P.R. last year. Luis Palau was the speaker. We then joined a little church called Holdbrook Christian Fellowship near Waltham Abbey and were baptised in the Holy Spirit. We have a truly lovely pastor who encourages us all to attend any Spirit-filled meetings that are taking place during the week if possible.

I think it was last November that he announced that the Reverend Trevor Dearing would be speaking at Ilford Pentecostal Church. (It was towards the end of the year, anyway.) He said that you were well worth hearing and that we should attend if possible and we'd be blessed.

So about half a dozen of us did. Your talk was about God being full of surprises — it was riveting! I'd never thought about that before. Then you started to minister to the sick, and although I'd read your book "Exit the Devil" I was still very sceptical when they all started going down like ninepins. I thought of every logical reason possible for it, i.e. a. They were being pushed. b. They were all suffering from mass hysteria. c. They were pretty sick anyway so they were fainting. d. They all felt they had to fall down so they were just doing it to oblige you!

Anyway, you then invited people who wanted a blessing to come to the front, so my husband and I joined the long queue — we weren't sick or anything but just wanted a touch from the Lord. As we shuffled along in the queue singing choruses I was thinking of two things. These were that I just wanted to touch the hem of Jesus' gown and that I definitely wasn't going to fall over. So you can imagine my absolute amazement when I got "slain in the Spirit" half-way down the church! I didn't even get to the front and have hands laid on! I could almost hear God chuckling and saying, "I'll show you a thing or two young lady". (Actually I'm not very young!) And you Trevor (I hope you don't mind me calling you Trevor because although you don't know us we think of you and Anne as very dear friends.) saw what had happened to me, and as you ministered to people you mentioned the woman who had just wanted to touch the hem of Jesus' gown!

So through you I got well and truly blessed that evening. The Lord dealt with my scepticism, He told me through you that I'd been thinking about the woman who touched the hem of Jesus' gown, and He gave me a surprise as a follow-up to your talk! What a lovely Lord we have.

But the blessings we have received through your ministry don't stop there, so I hope you don't mind if I go on to tell you of another one.

Until David and I became Christians last year there was only one committed Christian in our family, our sister-in-law Pearl. She had been a Christian for seven years and praying fervently for the rest of us, particularly her husband John who is David's elder brother. Shortly after David and I became Christians, David's younger brother Richard and his wife Diane also became Christians. They had seen the change in David and me and wanted to know all about it, which gave us a wonderful chance to explain to them, and they gave their lives to the Lord.

Well, by now the rest of us had added our prayers to Pearl's for John to be saved, and David and I kept saying that if only he could hear Trevor Dearing preach we were sure the Lord would speak to his heart through Trevor's ministry.

Except for David and me the rest of our family all live in the Loughborough area, so when we found out that you would be ministering at a place called Broughton Astley (or something similar) we thought it would be a real opportunity to take John to hear you. So we all prayed furiously for two weeks, firstly that John would agree to go, and secondly that he would be touched by your message Trevor.

Well, John did agree to go, so on the night in question David and I travelled up to Leicestershire to be there — we just knew that the Lord was going to answer our prayers — He had told us so very clearly during the previous days. What a lovely moment it was when John got out of his seat and came out to the front of that little church and gave his life to Jesus. If you remember seeing a little huddle of people all laughing and crying and praising the Lord — it was us.

122

So we praise Him and thank Him for the wonderful way in which He has touched our family, and we thank you Trevor and Anne for just being the way that you are and letting God use you in such a wonderful way. Your message on the night of John's conversion was on the Transfiguration. I remember how ill you looked that night Trevor, but I've never heard the Transfiguration preached on in such a wonderful way. How often the Lord uses us in spite of ourselves!

Carol Payne, October 1985.

# A Police Officer's Testimony

In 1976 I became a Christian due to me being a fanatical bookworm. I had noticed a new bookshop had opened in Uxbridge named "Maranatha", which meant nothing to me at the time. I went in and browsed around, and bought a book called "Exit the Devil" by Reverend Trevor Dearing. This happened on a Friday, I started reading it and continued it on the Saturday. I went to bed and read it until I fell asleep; I could not put it down as I was excited at what I was reading. I woke up on the Sunday morning and again started to read the book, then something happened that today thrills me, something that I will never be able to explain. Remember, I had never heard the name of Trevor Dearing until two days earlier.

I heard an inner voice say, "Turn the radio on." I had a small radio next to my bed, so I turned it on. I then had the urge to change the station to Radio London (all this seemed quite natural at the time). Then I heard the words, "At 11 a.m. the globe-trotting Exorcist, Trevor Dearing, will be here to answer your questions in a phone-in programme".

It then hit me what had happened. I jumped out of bed and ran downstairs to my Mother and tried to explain what had happened, feeling very frustrated that she would not be able to believe me.

123

At 11 a.m. my Mother and myself listened to the programme and became more interested in Christianity. In the next few days, I went to a small eating house for some lunch at mid-day, where I started chatting to a young woman. After a short while she told me that she was a nanny and that she had moved down from Tyne and Wear. She informed me that she had telephoned her mother the night before and told her she was homesick, lonely and was going to give her job up and return home. Her mother was a Christian and told her that she was going to a prayer meeting that night and she would pray that she would meet someone. The next day she met me.

I then told her about my experience with the radio and the book. She told me she was a Christian and began to explain a lot of things to me about the Bible and Christianity. I then contacted Trevor Dearing and was invited to Hainault in Essex, where I became a Christian.

Over the past twelve months I have been led by God to study a one year course in Apologetics with a Bible College (apologetics are a defence of the Christian faith) and then go on studying to find out the evidence for Christianity. I now go and speak in youth clubs and schools when I get the opportunity, and try to show that the evidence for our faith is abundant. I encourage them to investigate the evidence for themselves.

The atheist makes a statement: "There is no God". But when asked to produce the "evidence" they cannot. On the other hand, the person who acquaints himself or herself with the evidence for historical Christianity no longer has to take, as some would like to think, a blind leap, but can take an intellectual leap of faith.

I have had the pleasure of leading officers and members of their families to this knowledge. Our God has left us abundant evidence for His existence and that of His Son, Jesus Christ. As police officers of all people, we should be trained to seek the evidence.

# Keith
*Trevor recalls:*

He was a young scientist with a problem. When I first met Keith I found that the young man wanted to put God under a microscope and examine Him. He believed in facts — not miracles.

His philosophy seemed to be, "If God can't be fitted onto a viewing slide, He doesn't exist."

Time, however, was running out for agnostic Keith, and it started shortly after he and his lovely wife Marion moved to a private estate close to St Paul's, and Peter, a road surveyor, became their lodger.

Peter, a committed Christian, had a burning zeal to win others for Christ, and he began witnessing to Keith and Marion. Marion responded and accepted Christ, and she started attending St Paul's. But Keith couldn't see why he should put his trust in Jesus as his Saviour. He was a kind, sincere and loving man — but his attitude seemed to be: "I must have proof or I can't accept what you say is true. I'm a trained scientist, Vicar, and I need proof before I will accept anything."

I tried to explain that faith, not proof, is the main ingredient of Christianity, but Keith couldn't swallow that.

"It really works," I tried to explain, "I know from first-hand experience." But he firmly retorted, "I must have the evidence."

That night I left Keith's trim home after midnight, feeling sadly disturbed that my words had had no apparent effect on him at all. Having seen so many mighty miracles already, I had almost come to believe that I just had to open my mouth and another would take place there and then. It was God telling me it was His power, not mine.

Just when I was despairing over Keith's conversion, my friend Peter Scothern came into the picture. Keith and Marion agreed to give him a bed in their home during one of his missions at St Paul's. And Keith, being the gentleman he was, said he would attend one of Peter's meetings, mainly out of good manners. Then, at the meeting Keith began to find a strange stirring inside his heart which he couldn't explain in scientific terms.

And when Peter made an "altar call" for those who wished to accept Christ as their Saviour, Keith found a battle raging deep inside him. He couldn't explain why, but his legs took him to the front of the church where he stood with a crowd of others.

He mouthed the salvation prayer that the evangelist prayed for them to follow, but he couldn't understand what on earth he was doing there, in front of all these people. On returning to his seat he felt strangely let down that nothing spectacular had happened. He felt he had done his bit, and yet God had done nothing to satisfy his scientific longings.

But Keith was soon out front again, this time to receive prayer for the baptism of the Holy Spirit. As he stood in line, he said to God: "Lord, I do want to believe. If you are real and do exist, will you show me in some unforgettable and tangible manner."

Hardly had the prayer left his lips when he keeled over backwards and crashed to the floor like a fallen tree. His head hit against the wooden floor with great force, but it seemed that God had put an invisible cushion there, because he was not injured. He lay there helpless for about a minute and then rose up — a new man in Christ. It was like Saul's dramatic experience on the road to Damascus. Only he and God knew what went on in his heart as he lay there. But when he stood up his face glowed and he was obviously transformed.

126

But the story doesn't end there. Keith and Marion had two children, but wanted more. Marion was told by her doctor that it would be highly dangerous to have another, but she decided to "trust the Lord", and she conceived again. Then she began exhibiting all the terrifying symptoms the doctor had predicted. She went into hospital and I visited her there.

"Vicar," she said, "would you please pray for a miracle. I want this child and I believe that God can intervene in this matter."

So, in the ward, I laid hands on her and prayed for her miracle. After that Marion had a trouble-free pregnancy. She wasn't sick at all, and when she later went into the hospital labour ward, the staff began preparing the operating theatre for her expected terrible difficulties. But she had a natural childbirth — in half an hour, and was the first in her ward out of hospital. Since then Marion has even had a fourth child.

Keith went on to train for ordination to the Church of England ministry at a Cambridge theological college, and became an Anglican clergyman working in the south of England. It was a case of science and faith colliding in a sincere man — and faith winning through. Jesus claimed His own.

\* \* \* \* \* \* \* \* \* \* \* \* \* \* \* \* \* \* \* \* \* \* \* \*

One letter that we received declared:

"I felt life was hardly worth living. Your wife invited me to one of your Tuesday meetings. Praise the Lord! I am free! My Christian life is no longer a duty but a joy. I have witnessed the power of the Holy Spirit in a way I never imagined was possible today."

Another woman whose life was changed was Jean, from Hainault. Trevor had taken a group from St Paul's at the beginning of his ministry there, to Hyde Valley Pentecostal

127

Church, to see the Holy Spirit in action. Trevor was called upon to lay hands, for the first time, on people for healing.

All her life Jean had been a sincere yet formal worshipper and believer; first in her native Scotland, and then later in London.

As the service drew to a close, deeply moved by all she had seen and heard, she felt impelled to acknowledge her need of Jesus as her Saviour and Lord. She came running forward in tears. Trevor prayed over her and she really came to know the Jesus she had served for so long. Her life was transformed.

# Delivered from alcohol addiction

A young woman in a pathetically fallen state of life who found the power of Jesus able to work a radical transformation, was Joan. She came to St Paul's, Hainault, looking for help. She was an alcoholic who said she used men in order to get money for drink, and allowed them to use her for sexual gratification.

"What can you do to help me?" was her urgent question as she stood in front of the crowded church. "I have had a baby, the only thing in the world that I really love, and today the health authorities took the little girl away from me, because they say I'm unfit to look after her."

Joan was shaking with emotion as she spoke. She looked haggard, twice the age that she actually was, with greying hair and a furrowed brow. The way of life into which her alcoholism had driven her had exacted a terrible toll.

"I urge you to accept Jesus as your Saviour tonight and to put your complete trust in Him to save you," Trevor said. "He is able to meet your every need."

Joan said that she would trust Jesus the best way she knew how, and was taken into the counselling room to be further prayed for and helped. Later that night she was taken into the home of one of the caring members of our congregation, who accepted her and sought to help her. After a few weeks Joan testified to the church that she knew that Jesus had delivered her from her alcoholism and saved her from a life of continuing prostitution. It was not long before the health authorities saw an evident change in her and soon restored the little girl to her mother, to be looked after and brought up in the Christian faith.

Joan eventually became an assistant matron in an Old People's Home and has been happily married to a fine Christian man who knows all about her past life. Jesus had worked a miracle of transformation in her.

# A changed prisoner

Tony's problems were different from those of Joan; he was not an addict when he came to St Paul's; he was in fact a prisoner on the run from the police. He had escaped from Armley jail in Leeds and had fled to London, where the police were on the look-out for him. It was a cold and wet Tuesday evening when Tony saw the lights of the church shining brightly and heard the loud singing of praises to the Lord.

"The police will never look for me inside a church," he thought.

That evening Trevor was preaching about the love of God for every individual in the world, no matter how sinful they had become. Jesus, he declared, had died for everyone. Tony had never heard this before, and certainly had never known that God really loved him, just as he was. The immeasurable love of God came home to his heart and, when the invitation was made, he went forward to accept Jesus as his Saviour and Lord. He was counselled by one of the Christian helpers, and was determined to begin a new life.

He immediately gave himself up to the police and was taken back to prison to complete his sentence. There he gathered a group of fellow-prisoners around him to study the Bible. He led several of them to a personal knowledge of Jesus' saving work on the cross, one of whom is a Pentecostal Pastor today. Tony himself was released early because of his good behaviour. Friends from St Paul's kept in touch with him all the time, and eventually he became a city missionary, working for the Lord.

Another man who had been in prison, but had completed his sentence by the time he came to one of our Tuesday evening meetings, was Bryan. He was in a state of deep depression. It had been a degrading and humiliating experience to go to prison for fraud, because he was a "respectable" middle-class man. His business had gone into liquidation and he was an undischarged bankrupt.

His first marriage had ended in divorce, and his second "common law" marriage had also come to an end. He had no friends, money or home; in fact he had nothing left at all for which to live. He planned to commit suicide. However, at the service he heard about the power of Jesus to transform every circumstance and situation of life, and he went forward for ministry. At last, he felt there was hope. His heart was filled with joy and peace, and a new life began for Bryan at that very time, as he trusted in the Lord.

He began a Christian ministry which brought blessing to thousands. All his circumstances were completely reversed and he is now married to a lovely, dependable Christian wife with whom he experiences real happiness.

Not only is our own life miraculously transformed; so are our relationships — broken ones are miraculously restored:

Marguerite writes: "By way of an amazing Divine plan, I found myself at the end of August at St Paul's Cliftonville for Friday evening, Saturday morning and Saturday evening. At the end of Saturday morning I spoke to you, Anne, and we sat in a pew and prayed. You may or may not remember.

"I had been apparently cracking up and the Lord used just about everything that Trevor was teaching on, on all three occasions. It was as if it had all been arranged just for me. A message and interpretation and suddenly laying me out on the floor. Trevor was nowhere near me, nor were the catchers, however I have the thud on tape as a reminder of God's power.

"The tenderness and compassion and mercy in the preaching — I have never heard such a beautiful gentle ministry, and received such emotional healing that weekend.

"You may remember, Anne, that God was saying He had opened the prison door, and I could either go out or back to a life of misery. Well, I went out, and that really dealt the final death blow to Satan in hindering my Christian life. I am all the time conscious of breathing the fresh clean air 'outside', and although a Christian 7½ years, for the first time ever, I am enjoying being alive!

"My children, too, sufferers of my damaged being, are being restored. Hallelujah, what a Saviour! The most difficult thing was the false crutches and self-protective layers of self-deception, but I imagine many do not get through this sort of thing. Jesus has set me free!"

So also marriages, sometimes in danger of complete breakdown, are made anew as the couple become "one flesh" in Jesus:

# A marriage restored

"It was so lovely to meet you at Launde Abbey [where Trevor usually holds a week of teaching and healing ministry in the summer most years] and to learn so much from you.

"I came to you to tell you about my husband who had left home and was living in adultery. I had been praying so hard (with lovely Christian sisters) that the Lord would save him and bring him home. Until Launde I'd cried every time I'd thought and prayed about John (my husband) and the Lord would wake me several times in the night to pray for him. (Me that usually was lost deep in sleep from 10.30 pm to 6.30 am.)

"After Launde I didn't cry again, nor was I awakened in the night. BUT last night my husband came home and I'm just praising the Lord and had to write to tell you.

"I thank the Lord for making you you, with your wonderful sense of humour and your great love for everyone.

"The Lord bless you and encourage and strengthen both you and your lovely wife."

V.B.

# An American marriage beautifully restored

Anne remembers: A good number of years ago some American friends sent me a copy of the widely circulated *Guideposts* magazine in which is related the wonderful change that occurred in a man's life in Saybrook, when Trevor and I were missioning in America a few years previously. It seems that Paul had many problems which had resulted in marital separation. However, his wife Deb had found Christ and the union had been somewhat shakily restored. She longed for her husband to find the Saviour, for she knew that in Him lay the only hope of a permanent solution. She wrote:

Then a visiting clergyman from England, the Rev-erend Trevor Dearing, came to our Church. I thought Paul might be interested in hearing a speaker from another part of the world. But when I told Paul about Father Dearing I could see the old fire in his eyes and I quickly backed off.

However, on the following Sunday, as I was leaving for Church, Paul stopped me at the door. "I'll go with you," he said, adding quickly, "but just this once."

I was elated, but hid my feelings. Once in Church I could sense his resistance to everything that was taking place. He sat there stiff, scowling, silent when the hymns were sung. He heard the call to the altar, watched people answer it. Then, to my amazement, Paul rose slowly and moved down the aisle. "Oh Lord, he needs Your help," I prayed. But when the clergyman placed his hands on Paul's head, he just stiffly stood there, turned and hurried back to my side.

On the way home he was silent for a time, then quietly said, "I walked down the aisle because I wanted to cleanse myself of all the wrong I did and the hurt I gave you. But when Father Dearing put his hands on my head I was skeptical that anything could happen. Deb, I just couldn't open my heart."

I prayed for the right words to say. "Will . . . will you come with me again?" I ventured.

"Maybe. I don't know." And then he added almost under his breath, "I've watched you over the past year, Deb, and you've become so sure, so serene. I wish I could feel the way you do."

The following Sunday night Paul decided on his own to attend the prayer meeting in Church. Father Dearing and his wife, Anne, were at the altar. When Father Dearing began talking, Paul listened intently. He hunched forward when Father Dearing talked of our inner prison, a prison of our own making. We all want to escape it, but even the most powerful cannot escape alone. There is only One who can give us the key. Then he invited everyone who had not yet met Jesus to come and meet Him.

Paul stood up. His face was pale, his eyes shining, his fingers gripped my arm. "Deb, come with me," he said softly. I rose and he placed me in front of him, still holding my arm. We followed the first few people down the aisle. At the altar he stood behind me. I heard a noise. I turned. Paul lay on the floor. People were praying over him. Then he got up slowly and led me back to our seats. He was alright but I was mystified as to what had happened to him.

When the meeting was over Paul hurried both of us outside.

"I wasn't sure anything would happen," he said, his face flushed, his speech rapid, as though he wanted to tell it all at once.

"But when Mrs Dearing put her hands on my head, I felt a surge of peace sweep through me like a big ocean wave. All my strength left me. Next thing I knew I was on my back, looking up at a ring of faces praying. My mind cleared, and I knew I had surrendered myself to the presence of God."

Paul's face was filled with a new light. He looked serene, at peace. He crushed me to him and said huskily, "Deb, I felt as if I was resting in the hands of the Lord!"
"You were, Paul," I said joyously. "You are!"

134

Since that day, God's hand has been on Paul. His inner turmoil is gone. Of course, our problems didn't all disappear, nor did our marriage become all sweetness and light. But now the two of us are working on them together.

*(Guideposts*, August 1985)

# A miner's story

K.E. writes: "In 1971-72 darkness and despair hit my life. I had an operation to my right knee, and after the operation a blood clot stopped in my right lung and made me very poorly. I began to get better slowly after treatment, but being young I thought I must push myself hard to get back on my feet, all the while struggling.

"I found I had trouble going out, and I had to have tablets to stop vertigo. I could only think of dying. The doctor laughed at me and said I wouldn't die; he didn't know how I felt. All the time I kept trying to go, but heaviness held me back.

"After about five months off work I started back. I found I could no longer work underground at the pit, so a job was found for me on the surface. I still lost a lot of time off work. I just didn't want to go. Then I looked at my family I had to keep: two boys and a wife; later we had a third child, also a boy. I had to keep going to show I was not idle, and be an example to them, but I was still struggling.

"Then I took to drink. I could drive the car better and felt lifted until the morning, which is why I lost time at work. I had an affair with another woman and nearly destroyed my marriage, but glory to God He kept my wife strong, and she forgave me in her way.

"My employer sent for me and gave me three months to improve my attendance. This was at the colliery I started from school. I had truly loved my work underground before my illness, and with this news I was very worried, so I tried again to keep going, but all in vain.

"So it was back to the doctor's; a lady doctor, not my normal one. I broke down in the surgery, saying I just could not go on with my job. She gave me a three-week sick note, one of many. I came home lost, but I knew I could not give up. I was taking nerve tablets to help me, but the drinking did not cease, and I was taking both.

"In the first week off work a neighbour came in to see my wife, and when I shared with her about work and finding a new job, she suggested I tried Silverhill Colliery where her husband worked. I did, and a miracle happened. A man had put in his notice at Silverhill Colliery to go and work at the colliery I was at, therefore I got the new employment.

"A fresh start, but it wasn't long before the old way of life returned: not wanting to work. Shortly after this I got put to work with a Christian. He told me he knew about the mess I was in and he asked me, after sharing his faith with me, if I would like to go to the church where he worshipped.

"I didn't go the first weekend, but on the following Sunday I just ached with pain, and instead of lying in bed, which I loved to do, I had no peace; I had to get up. I went to the Church of St John the Baptist at Tibshelf, which is about six miles from my home. This is where God has put me to serve Him. That same morning I gave myself to Christ.

"Shortly afterwards I heard about your meeting at Matlock from people of the church, so we went by car, my wife and I and two friends. I went out to God's call and was set free.

"I don't now take tablets for nerves; I have been healed inwardly. I don't drink, I can go to work regularly and I have the strength to face the day. It is a challenge; I do still have problems but I do have a peace which only God can give, and this helps me in my daily life.

"I do thank you both for being vessels for God and the work He is doing through you both."

*Quite a miracle!*

# A somewhat milder deliverance

From K.C.: "I am writing to thank you for the blessing I received from the Lord through Anne's prayer and laying on of hands at Corby. My prayerful thanks were delayed in case the change in me, through lack of faith on my part, was temporary.

"Apart from inevitable periods of abstinence during the war and for six months after I was converted in 1960 (aged 38) I have been a daily drinker of beer. So this was a daily habit for decades.

"Without realising it I was drinking to excess and suffered some health breakdown, causing me to stop working at 63 years old. Financial cramp and health limitations forced me to cut back considerably — but I was still enjoying two large cans of 9% proof lager a day; a habit broken only by weekly forays to seek out 'real ale'.

"I asked Anne to pray for healing for back trouble — which cleared up in its time — but she also prayed for my general health. The next morning I didn't want my lager ration, and felt the same way the following morning. It then occurred to me that this was the Lord helping me to help myself. So with prayerful thanks I did not have any alcohol until I went out with a friend for a pub lunch. I just had one drink.

"I now find that I can, without any mental effort or effort of will on my part, do without alcohol.

"So thank you both, and praise the Lord Jesus for His merciful intervention through His Holy Spirit — healer and comforter."

# Also Michael

A Pastor writes: "Just a word about Michael. He has attended our church on and off for about a year. He has had a major drink problem. He was given drugs to help him kick it but he ended up taking the drugs and drinking at the same time. About two months ago he was at an all time low and was really in a sorry state. He had a Church of England background, but I was never quite sure if he was really saved.

"He came forward for prayer the night you came, and told me he felt an electric current go right through him. He has not been the same since. After I had preached on the Sunday after your visit, he came forward and unconditionally gave his life to the Lord! He has not touched the drink since."

After our mission in Singapore in 1992 we received a letter from Ivor and Rosemary Williams:

"My wife (Rosemary) and I were in Singapore in September on our way to visiting our extended families in Australia.

"On Sunday 2 September I asked my hotel porter for the way to the nearest RC church. He directed me across the road to St Andrew's Cathedral. I felt sure that he was mistaken but nevertheless went there, to find that a World Evangelical Congress was about to start.

"That night, after mass at the RC cathedral, we went to the first of your three evening meetings. We also went to the second and third, and have the tapes of all three. We now see ourselves as 'Born Again Catholics' and have had the opportunity, in our local church, to make our witness for Christ as co-leaders of a diocesan Renew programme. As the topic was Evangelisation, we had every chance to remind people of the Good News which some of them had forgotten.

"After the Singapore congress we were fortunate enough to meet and spend some time with the Rev Alan Maddox (from Western Australia) who was on an exchange visit to Singapore. He helped us a great deal. But we had wanted to get in touch with you. I have just got your address through the Evangelical Alliance.

"We specially want to thank you and your wife Anne for the wonderful events of Singapore, which have changed our lives dramatically.

"In Brisbane it was a great joy to us to be at one with our daughter's family, who are RC Charismatics and 'in the Kingdom', as you put it. So their prayers on our behalf had been answered, as had those of our youngest son, who is a member of Cobham Christian Fellowship.

"(PS: My wife stood up on Night 1. It took me another two days, but I made it on Night 3! I shall be 70 on Christmas Day — it will be very special.)"

# Lois, Newport, Gwent:

"I want to say how much I enjoyed Anne's book — her gentle spirit of joy radiates from the pages together with a purity of character not often met these days. Thank you for sharing so openly and honestly your story.

"Your ministry has made so much difference to my former wretched life and I have found that <u>Peace</u> from God. I will always be so grateful for Eileen Mohr who, when we lived in Harlow, brought me to Hainault for healing and salvation. I experienced the perfume of the Holy Spirit on my first visit — a rare gift from the Lord in my rebellious and distressed state as a single (divorced) parent.

"Through your ministry there I brought my children to the Lord, and they are saved. Praise God!"

# Rosemary, Oakham

"Praise the Lord! I am actually living a new life since the Lord, through you, obtained for me the healing I so needed and desired. It is early days as yet, but even so I feel that I should like to live to 101 in order that my prayer of thanksgiving shall grow, and my praise reach around this planet.

"His mercy is so sure that we can wear it as a garment; it makes us impervious to catastrophe and crisis, and for people like me, especially me — subject to changes of mood and rhythm which are such a plaguish thing when one is trying to live a normal life.

"That part of your address which dealt with the healing of the whole person I particularly noted, as I feel that however legion symptoms may be, they are *only indications of being out of step with Him.* I shall strive to be a wholly new person in outlook as in mental well-being, and to love Him and all people as I ought.

"May He bless your work and healing hands, and those of your wife."

*Reflecting on his own conversion and healing, Trevor writes:* Conversion to Christ is the process by which a self divided and distraught becomes united, integrated and happy under the impetus of a dynamic religious experience. This was certainly true in my own experience at the age of nineteen, and I have also had the privilege of seeing the same process take place in the lives of hundreds of people to whom I have since ministered. It has been the reality of a deep relationship with God which has brought wholeness to their minds and emotions.

A typical example was that of J.T., a woman who was living at Waltham Abbey, Hertfordshire. She described her experience as follows:

"My nerves and agoraphobia started when I was nineteen. I spent most of my days sitting on a chair holding on to a fireguard, scared even to walk across the room. I came to the Lord about three years ago. Isn't it a lovely thought to know that Jesus accepts us for what we are and then remoulds us. What a friend!

"Well, I decided that after fourteen years of treatment I no longer needed a psychiatrist, because I have the promise that Jesus will make me well. So last week I went to my hospital therapy group and said that I didn't need to come any more. The psychologist knew that I had been receiving Divine healing, and gave me half an hour to tell the group about it.

"In difficult times I listen to tapes and have a really good chat with the Lord, and find real peace in Him."

So, if you, dear reader, want to experience this miraculously transformed life, then say sorry to God for all your past failures, mistakes — 'sins', believe that this transformation has been made possible by the life, death upon the cross and resurrection of Jesus. Then ask Jesus to take all your life, in all its respects, into His hands and transform it by the life within you of His Holy Spirit.

It is very simple. The only qualification for which He asks is to feel your need of Him. Do this. Join a lively church fellowship. Read your Bible (you may prefer one of the modern translations). Pray every day, and a new life is yours in time and eternity.

# Miracles in Brief

*The following are instances of healing miracles described very briefly:*

First of all, some
Miracle Babies — *babies born to parents who had difficulty with conception or pregnancy* :

**Christine-Louise Rebecca,** born 30 September 2000, "result of prayer from April 1999 when Trevor prayed for us. Praise the Lord! God is good."

**David Alexander John,** born 7th February, weighing 7lb 4oz.

**Penny, born to Anna and Roger,** even though Anna had lost one tube and the other was badly blocked. She had many operations, and was told to forget her wish to have a baby; but Penny was born, after prayer. Anna writes, "the doctors had a shock".

**B. and J.** write: "After three IVF attempts we discovered that I had conceived quite naturally. We are expecting a baby at the end of March. Thanks once again for your prayers and ministry."

**The Rev Daniel Foot** wished to say 'thank you' to the Lord for healing his back through Trevor's ministry at Kettering. He had damaged his back moving furniture, and before ministry could not walk upstairs.

**"The lady** whose legs were affected has had no recurrence at all of her problems, and my ulcerative colitis has been completely clear since you prayed over us. We thank our wonderful God that He used you to touch us."

Liverpool: **"One lady** has reported that she was healed of a heart condition . . . she attended hospital the following week for tests . . . it was found that a heart by-pass was not required. Praise the Lord!"

*The following are some of the miracles resulting from the prayers of the Fellowship of Intercessors, mentioned in Chapter 6:*

G. P. — her health has improved enormously, since prayer — she is no longer having the severe asthmatic attacks which have kept her indoors for such long periods — praise the Lord!

M. H .— shares that her blood test is now normal — the biopsy on the artery above her eye was clear, and the whole eye perfect!

A. L — very grateful for prayer — he is already responding to the course he knows the Lord has 'arranged' for him in the special Compressor unit for multiple sclerosis patients — he is less stiff down his left side, and is finding walking easier — he hasn't yet had half the course, so is really praising the Lord!

Mrs. J. E. shares with great joy that the skin cancer on her mother's face has been completely healed, medically confirmed, following prayer!

S. T. for whom we prayed sometime ago in the Fellowship has been completely healed of pre-menstrual tension and feels 'on top of the world' she is very grateful to all who prayed for her.

D. H. — very grateful for prayer she has now regained the confidence she lost through the trauma of fracturing both femurs, and can drive her car again!

C. A. — very grateful for prayer "I managed to go for a lovely walk up our country lane for the first time, after many months of being 'housebound' ".

*Miracles in brief*

Mrs. M. H. — has been seriously ill with rare wasting disease, myasthenia gravis and bad heart and eye problems —she shares: "'I am gradually gaining strength after my wonderful recovery which can only be attributed to the strength of prayer. I positively felt this on the day everyone expected to be my last! I also felt deeply at peace — obviously although 'rising 80' there is work for me to do!'"

B. G. — shares that her diabetic condition has now become stable after the trauma of further surgery for repair of her bladder. Her arthritic condition has also improved, and she has actually been able to ride her bicycle again — would appreciate continued prayer for complete wholeness!

P. D. — her son Adrian has 'taken on a new lease of life and is enjoying his job on a farm' — he was agoraphobic, so Pat is praising the Lord for answered prayer!

P. P. — very grateful for prayer — her daughter Alison has made a wonderful recovery from anorexia nervosa and her elder daughter Nirree is completely healed; no further migraine and has been off all tablets for several weeks — praise God.

G. M. — very grateful for prayer — the tablets taken for her very severe headaches have been reduced from 63 per week to 9—14 'this is super, some days I can go for 24 hrs without taking any'.

P. B. — thanks all who prayed for their daughter — her baby arrived safely. She has now been converted, and attends a Baptist Church. Her husband (an ex— skinhead) has been converted whilst in Dartmoor Prison. He is now a 'model prisoner' and is hoping to get parole soon, and knows the Lord has work for him to do; perhaps amongst his former 'skinhead' friends.

146

N. N. — shares great improvement in young Angela (had very severe asthma) after prayer — she no longer has to wear the special instrument over her head and shoulders. She rides her bicycle, swims and has joined the Church Brownies — praise the Lord!

A. P. — is very grateful for prayer — the Lord has now brought her off all the tablets she had been taking since the loss of her husband, and she says: 'Jesus set me free from the desire to take them — my mind is so much clearer. I didn't realise how doped I had become.'.

J. M. — shares the good news that her sister is now home from hospital where she received a 'double miracle' — her colostomy was successfully 'reversed', and she had been told that she had cancer, which is now completely healed — praise the Lord!

Mrs. M. — very grateful for prayer — they are praising the Lord that although 'symptoms were very distressing and were those of cancer' — results of both x—rays and biopsy were negative!

Mrs. J. S. — shares the wonderful news that her nephew Peter, who had been given 3-5 months to live after surgery for removal of a malignant brain tumour, is now (3 months on) well and on holiday in Germany with his father's sister and family! He is now planning to look for work on their return — 'is not at all depressed and is convinced that God is dealing with the problem and that all will be well'! She shares that this whole experience has drawn all the family much closer together, and they have been much comforted by our prayers, for which they are very grateful.

Mr. P. — for whom we prayed for healing of emphysema is 'now out of hospital and although rails and ramps have had to be fitted, at least he is home' — he is very grateful for our prayers — praise the Lord!

147

B. L. — shares that she had the privilege of praying for an elderly lady who had collapsed during the night, on their return flight. 'Within 20 minutes she was quiet, the doctor was smiling and the oxygen mask etc. were taken of'. They were very grateful for our undergirding prayer throughout.

Mrs. W. — her sister—in—law Marjorie had a very large brain tumour removed — it was benign and not malignant, as had been expected — praise the Lord! She is making good progress.

A. M. — shares gratitude for prayer and encouraging news — 'I'm delighted to say the recent test shows that my blood now has a normal iron level! I also believe some healing has taken place re the brain damage problem — I'm beginning to remember to do things, and can write letters with greater ease.'

Mrs M. W. — prayer is being wonderfully answered — she is now able to eat again and is very much better in herself — she is trusting the Lord for a complete miracle.

Mrs S. O. is very grateful for our prayers, love and caring — she was a 'bag of nerves', but since receiving the anointed prayer cloth, which she requested, she is very much better, and able to get out and about again — praise the Lord!

Dr. A. M. — very grateful for prayer which has been speedily answered. All pain in her knees has gone, and she no longer needs to take any tablets! Their recently adopted baby Sarah (3 months premature and with a severe chest complaint) is now flourishing.

Mrs. B. M. — shares wonderful answered prayer for her daughter Gillian (handicapped) — 'she is settling in to her work as co—leader at "The Parsonage" in a manner which I think is a God—given way. She is experiencing His strength and is very happy !'

148

Paul D. — (already healed of cancer, following prayer) writes 'I am now back at work on full duties, and cycling an 18 mile round trip twice weekly — in many ways I'm now more than 100% fit because other minor ailments (skin condition, cramps, depression and sore gums) have also been healed! My mother (arthritis and osteoporosis in her legs) has received an "overnight" touch from the Lord in all her joints and her "bad" ankle — for which surgery had been advised. — She can now climb stairs, using both legs, which she hasn't been able to do for a year!'

Norman and Ethel Dudgeon share wonderful news re their ministry to mainland China — Brother Yu Han was imprisoned in the 1950s and was concerned re his 3 congregations (300 members altogether). On his release in 1978 these had grown to 20 congregations (5000 Christians!) Christ Himself had looked after his sheep and caused them to grow.
Now in 1985 each congregation has over 1000 members, a total of 20,000 Christians!'

Mrs. June Hawkes — shares wonderful news re Joan H. — 'she has been notified by the hospital that the cancer has cleared from her body — it's a miracle of the Lord!'

N. N. — very grateful for prayer for E. (whose eyesight was failing through the lights in the factory) — everything is now well again, and he won't have to lose his job!'

Mrs. J. H. — shares continued progress in answer to prayer — 'My allergy is stable, the tests show a big improvement, and I'm able to add more items of food to my meagre diet, which is very encouraging!'

B. M. — shares answered prayer for Christine P. — 'the melanoma was safely removed from her leg, and she had a skin graft which healed up perfectly in under a month!'

149

Mrs E. P. — shares continued answer to prayer: 'all swelling has gone from my ankles (— enormous before!) and my life has been transformed since coming to the Lord Jesus — I can now walk with new strength and confidence, in Him.'

G. W. — shares thrilling news re John Ward — "the Specialist has confirmed that there is no sign of Cushing's Syndrome (pituitary gland problem) — his rnother is 'over the moon' that they can find nothing wrong with him !"

A. S. — 'I had a bad attack of shingles recently, but knowing you were all praying for me I didn't have the pain the doctor expected, and didn't need any of the strong painkillers given to me — I really am feeling much better!'

J. H. — writes that. miraculously her mother **(92)** had a temporary and then a permanent pacemaker fitted — 'amazing that this was even attempted!'

E. K. — shares answered prayer for Jonathan (who was so ill for such a long time) — 'he suddenly began to eat and drink in a normal way, read a book and watch T.V.! It has been 3 years of agony for his family, seeing him in a wheelchair and being force—fed. "The Lord has given him a wonderful miracle — he is now back at school, and recently took a cup of tea to his parents in bed, for a surprise." — Praise the Lord indeed!'

Arthur F. — we have just heard that he continues to make excellent progress after his healing from cancer (following prayer) — he comes through his regular medical checks with flying colours.

Dr R. C. — shares answered prayer for young Thomas. 'His parents appropriated the anointed prayer cloth you sent — Thomas had 9 fits and was very bad for the first day. Since then there have been whole days without a single fit! The main thing is he is looking much brighter and is more lively in himself. His parents feel something is happening.'

T. and S. T. — say that Lynne (who had a cyst growing inside her which disappeared following earlier prayer!) 'has given birth to a bonny baby boy' — Praise God! Also Elizabeth's father 'has made a miraculous recovery, and to look at him you would never think he had been so close to death and seeing Jesus — He knows best!'

A. C. — shares wonderful answers to prayer — "the tinnitus etc. was going to the other ear as well, but after putting the prayer cloth you sent under my pillow, the 'noise' had left the 'good' side by morning! I then asked for tests and all was perfect — no damage done — it's a miracle! The Lord has also healed me from a phobia from which I've suffered for many years!"

A. C. — 'My back is definitely improving, and the blood pressure and blood salt condition was healed gradually, enabling my normal vitality to be restored.'

C. O. — shares joyfully that his mother Gwyneth is 'now blooming with health, and free from all arthritis — her blood pressure is also under control' — praise the Lord!

Mrs B. F. shares: 'I am now back at work, and although still rather weak and tired, it has been such a comfort knowing you were all praying for me! So many nice things are happening now, usually when I most need them (like your letter assuring me of the prayers of the Fellowship) arriving the day after my really low one, when I felt I couldn't survive another — but I DID! My son is less depressed and now looking for work.'

C. W. — says: 'the most important thing that has happened recently is that I've invited the Lord Jesus into my heart! This was followed by a Word of Knowledge re someone with angina whom God wanted to heal, and I knew it was me! I have been feeling much better — most of my pains and morbid fears have gone, I've stopped losing weight and am now off all tablets

151

(except one to help with sleep at night) — I long for the day when I'm completely well and can show others what God has done for me.'

B. M. shares that her friend Mavis 'has now completely recovered from her depression — apart from the odd twinge, the hip which she injured is now much better and she has been able to return to her nursing job.'

Mrs. D. — gives thanks for prayers 'which have changed my son Ranjit a lot! He was expected to be in hospital for 2 months, but he only needed 2 weeks and is healed!'

Margot H. shares wonderful answered prayer for Hilary — 'despite having been thrown through the windscreen of the car, and being in Intensive Care with multiple serious injuries, she is now completely healed and back at work!'

P. J. — gives some interesting news re answered prayer in the early days of the Fellowship of Intercessors: 'You sent me an anointed prayer cloth for the healing of lumbago — quite unbelieving, I put this at the base of my spine and all the pain went within 2 days, and stayed away until last October I actually found the prayer cloth, and the same result was forthcoming — certainly the Lord healed me!'

Sam Quigley — some further encouraging news has just come from the U.S.A. — "He has overcome the cancer that was diagnosed late in 1984, and recovered well from the side—effects of earlier treatment! His effective healing lifts a great load off all our hearts! He's returned to his work as keeper of the musical instrument collection at the Boston Museum of Fine Arts." Our prayers were greatly appreciated.

J. U. — shares that Janet (the alcoholic for whom we were praying) continues to make excellent progress — she is now receiving special counselling with which she couldn't previously have coped.

R. S. — says that she is very much better and knows our prayers and her patience 'resulted in complete removal of all depression and a new depth in her relationship with the Lord! Following recent investigations, all areas of her colon are clear and there is now no sign of the colitis which troubled her for so long.'

Mrs L. H. — shares: 'I have already had 2 very important reactions to your prayers — the first (and most wonderful) is that there has been a deep sense of peace that all is in the Lord's hands and under His control! The second is a progressive healing of the sore place on the toe joint, which made the wearing of a shoe so very painful.'

Mr and Mrs Tony Dawson — share further news regarding Chris W. (**M.S.**) — 'There has been further improvement and he continues to make good progress. He now has a much more positive attitude and increased spiritual strength — he also drives short distances and his family has cheered up and witnessed about God's power at every opportunity.'

J. G. — shares news of wonderfully answered prayer: 'Praise the Lord I have been completely healed — the lump in my groin has completely disappeared - I placed the anointed prayer cloth over it, as you advised, and commanded it to go, in the Name of Jesus – it's wonderful to be free!'

Mrs S. — gratefully shares news of continued answers to prayer — 'we really thank God that our son Trevor's drinking is now a thing of the past. We have been seeing much more of him and his wife after that long gap.'

J. P. — answered prayer — The goodness of the Lord and the sure knowledge that He was with me, following my recent heart attack, has increased and not diminished my faith! Whilst in Intensive Care He kept telling me: "This sickness is not unto death" and I knew all would be well! I now feel fit and well and stronger every day — His Grace is indeed sufficient — thank you once again for all your love and caring!'

Dr A. M. (U.S.A.) — shares wonderfully answered prayer for their 2 youngest adopted children Peter (18 months) and Matthew (14 months) both ex-Korean orphans who have been very seriously ill in the Mayo Clinic with rare conditions — both are now home and making excellent progress.'

M. G. — says: 'You will be thrilled to hear that my nephew Geoffrey, for whom you were praying (thoracic cancer) is now so well that he was able to take part in a long distance run, sponsored for charity, in his Army Depot - he has also stopped smoking - praise the Lord!'

B. F. — shares the lovely healing of Mary, following prayer — 'She had very severe pain and swelling from a lump on one finger — treatment had made this worse and surgery was being queried. After a Sunday morning Service (during which she couldn't concentrate because of the pain) she awoke 2 days later to find the lump had gone — the doctors were mystified and thought she'd gone mad when asked to re—examine a lump which had gone!'

T. J. – 'I thank you from the bottom of my heart for all your prayers — after many years of terrible agoraphobia and depression, I've literally seen a miracle happen within my inner self! Only a few weeks ago I was terrified to go to our local Post Office, and now I walk 6 miles a day without panic. My massive dosage of tablets is now so low that it's hardly worth bothering about! The Lord has enabled me to start training designed to get me back into employment - to Him be all the Glory!'

S. R. — shares: 'I delight in telling you that Jesus <u>has</u> healed my epilepsy - I'm now off all tablets after 5 years! He told me a year ago I would be cured, and the recent scan has now proved this — I <u>had</u> to spend those years in the wilderness for a purpose and He has all the glory — praise Him!' She sounded really delighted and so grateful for prayer!

E. M. - 'I had a hiatus hernia about 6 months ago and, with you, was believing the Lord for healing. A drink and biscuits were brought to me one evening whilst in the Nursing Home — as some were cream ones I asked the Lord what I should do and He said: "Eat them"! From that time I've gone back to normal food and given up all my tablets, for which I really praise the Lord! Folk keep looking at me in surprise and asking how I feel. I say "wonderful", and I've been free from all pain for two months. My love, blessings and many thanks to all who've prayed for me!'

# *Finally, from the publisher:*

When my husband and I lived in Harlow, Essex, I discovered what was happening in St Paul's, Hainault every Tuesday evening, and experienced the wonderful, almost tangible presence of Jesus, and miracles of healing.

We owned a 12-seater Land-Rover at the time, to cater for our family with four children, so I found myself frequently transporting people from Harlow to Hainault, who were seeking healing. By the time Trevor's ministry there came to an end, I added up how many people I had taken there. I remembered 31. Of that number, with the exception of one lady whom I didn't know well, and with whom I didn't keep in contact, each one had been healed.

Three cases stand out in my memory. One was my elderly friend, Ivy Prior. She was sitting next to me in the meeting, and when the healing ministry started, she whispered, "I'm going forward for my **arthritis.**"

Her hands had been crippled with arthritis for some years, so that she was unable to use a pair of scissors.

When she came back to her seat after ministry, she was stretching out the fingers of both hands and flexing them, **completely restored to normal flexibility.**

"Just like that!" she exclaimed with a mixture of triumph and wonderment.

The second was a young man who lived in the same road as us, whose face and body were covered with disfiguring **eczema.** He had tried all kinds of creams and ointments, including those prescribed by the doctor, but nothing had helped.

We were sitting near the front of the church on that occasion, so I heard Trevor praying for this young man. He said: "In the Name of Jesus, your skin will be perfectly well, as smooth as a baby's skin!"

And about two days later it had happened — his skin really was as smooth as a baby's.

The third outstanding healing was that of Grace Wildman. I didn't know her personally at the time, but she had phoned me a few weeks previously, asking me if I was going to Hainault. At that point I was too busy to go, and I made a note of her name and address, but not her telephone number. A few weeks later I was again arranging to take one or two friends along, and on the Monday prior to the meeting I felt a strong prompting to go to the address of the woman who had phoned, even though I didn't know her, and it was very inconvenient that day. So, ignoring the inconvenience, I drove to the woman's house, and asked her if she would like to go to Hainault the following evening.

Her reaction was: "Oh, that's wonderful! I've been told I've got **gallstones**, and I'll probably be in hospital over Christmas having an operation!"

I was sure the Lord had led me to invite her. After she had received ministry on the Tuesday evening, she said: "I heard the gallstones crunch as I was falling down to rest in the Spirit!" I shared her joy, both because she had been healed, and also would *not* be in hospital over Christmas.

To God be the glory!

E.M.

# Conclusion

Trevor first met the Lord Jesus when he was nineteen years of age, and has been serving Him in full-time ministry for fifty years. What a wonderful way in which to spend one's life. Anne has known Jesus since early childhood, and likewise has served Him all her life; with Trevor since 1957.

When Trevor was in theological college, he met up with the "God is Dead" theology which was prevalent, especially in the USA. The teaching was that God existed, but was dead to the world and mankind in that He never did anything to show that He existed! This was a reiteration of the theology of Deism with which John Wesley had contended in the 18th Century. It was believed by Deists that God had created the earth and mankind, then wound it up like a clock to "tick" its way to its end without any interference from Himself. — In other words He had, as it were, created — and then gone away!

This book has taught and portrayed a very different concept of God from all that. It has shown that God is a *living* God, totally active in human life as a whole and in individuals in particular, on condition that they believe in Him, seek Him, and open their lives to Him through means He has chosen to use.

This concept again is far removed from present-day "fundamentalist, evangelical dispensationalism", wherein sincere believers in Jesus and His salvation from sin, nevertheless believe that all the miraculous events we here

158

described, except the "changed life", are to be limited to Bible days and not expected to happen today.

The experiences of those who have testified to God's intervention in their lives today, not only through our ministry, but also many more, save on a much grander scale than ours, show the power of the living God. Multitudes are continuing to experience this in the same ways that we have described. World-wide testimony to these experiences of God abound in nearly every country, colour and tongue, and as Smith Wigglesworth once said,

> "The man with an experience is never at the mercy of a man with an opinion."

To this we say a heartfelt "Amen!"

# Index

The following are sicknesses or other conditions mentioned in healing miracles described in this book: